MW01225861

OYS Enterprises
Calgary AB, Canada
info@timrichardson.ca

Tim Richardson, author
Heather Morin, cover art

ISBN 978-1-9990714-1-7   Paperback
ISBN 978-1-9990714-0-0   eBook

First Edition

This is a work of nonfiction. Some names and identifying details have been changed.

OWN YOUR SH!T

FACING YOUR PAST TO DOMINATE YOUR FUTURE

TIM RICHARDSON

TABLE OF CONTENTS

"Taking responsibility means never blaming anyone else for anything you are being, doing, having, or feeling."

— **Susan Jeffers, Feel the Fear and Do It Anyway®: Dynamic techniques for turning Fear, Indecision and Anger into Power, Action and Love**

DEDICATION

To Annie, Cole, and Sidnee: I love you more than words can say. You are my guiding stars. You make every day the happiest day of my life.

To Mum and Dad: You didn't have much in the way of money, but you had an abundance of love to give. I love you, Mum. I miss you, Dad.

ACKNOWLEDGEMENTS:

Everyone needs great support while going through significant changes. I want to thank my wife and two incredible children for putting up with my unbelievable number of mistakes throughout my life and being patient time after time. My transformation couldn't have been done through the past eight years without you being there by my side every day.

I would also like to acknowledge Joanna D'Angelo, who is such a great listener and helped me organize my thoughts and my life to share with the world. A big thank you to Big Sky Author Services, and specifically Tammy Plunkett, for her guidance and patience throughout this whole process—you have been priceless throughout this adventure!

It is often said "it takes a village to raise a child," and these important people made up the village that helped shape my life: Peter Jennings, whose professionalism taught me to do the right thing at all costs, even when no one is looking or applauding you; Chuck Shields who took a chance on me, a 19-year-old kid; Murray Jenkins who introduced me to the world of entrepreneurialism and sales. A part of these three incredible men will be with me forever.

Lastly, I try and be proud of how I live every day but I also aim to make the following gentlemen proud as well: David Hames, whose calmness and common sense approach to life always help me make better decisions, and Joel Bray, whose life experiences make me never want to let him down.

Prologue

The Beginning of the End.

"If you always do what you've always done, you'll always get what you've always got."
— Susan Jeffers, *Feel the Fear and Do It Anyway*

"This is getting really old, Mr. Richardson."
I heard her words, but I didn't listen.
My wife, Annie. She is the reason I am here today. The reason I dug deep and took charge of my life. She is the reason I didn't end up six feet under.
It was going to be the best family vacation ever. Vegas baby! Annie and the kids and I were in Vegas for twelve days in the fall of 2011. Annie turned to me as we were unpacking the kids' clothes, refolding them and laying them in the drawers in their bedroom. "Do you think you can go for the entire vacation without drinking?"
"Of course, I can." I replied, defensive and angry that she would even ask. I shouldn't have been defensive. I should have been truthful. I was a "functioning alcoholic" but I couldn't admit it to myself. I got up and went to work every day. I worked hard. But at the end of the day I used alcohol to

"unwind". I also drank on weekends. At social occasions, I would drink to excess. I would drink to the point of making myself physically ill. I had been in denial for many years. My drinking was out of control. I was travelling a twisted and dangerous path and I was approaching the edge of a cliff and I didn't know how to keep from falling.

Cole, age 13, and Sidnee, age 12, were running around the sitting room, flicking on lamps, turning on the TV, opening the bar fridge, screaming in excitement.

"Mom, can I have a bag of chips?" Cole asked.

"Mom, can I have a chocolate bar?" Sidnee asked.

"We're going out for dinner in an hour. How about something to drink instead?" Annie answered closing the drawer.

I carried my shaving kit into the bathroom and slammed it on the counter. I was pissed off. Pissed that Annie had so little faith in me. I promised that I wouldn't drink. Why didn't she believe me? Because you made that promise a gazillion times before and you always end up drinking, my inner voice piped up. Geez! Well, there was a first time for everything, right? I wanted Annie and the kids to have a good time, so I promised I wouldn't drink. You don't have to drink to have a good time, right?

Annie was a little cool towards me at dinner, and watchful, like she was waiting for me to hail the server and order a beer or wine. When the server asked if we wanted a cocktail or wine with dinner, I shook my head and smiled. We ordered mineral water instead. But I couldn't shake my anger.

I was still stewing the next day. I'd arranged for a car service to drive us everywhere and we had a busy week planned, daily outings, concerts and shows. But I couldn't shake my anger and resentment. I wasn't going to drink. I would prove that to Annie. For the entire week I stayed away from booze. And then it happened.

It was our second to last night in Vegas. We'd had a great day capped off by a tour of the Grand Canyon. When we got back to the hotel, we talked about the thrill of seeing the majesty of the Canyon up close.

"Is that how a bumblebee feels like every day Daddy?" Sidnee asked me, her hazel eyes wide. We were relaxing in the sitting room in the hotel suite munching on burgers and fries. Sunshine streamed through the windows of the suite. The kids didn't feel like going to dinner, so we'd ordered room service.

"I think you're exactly right Sidnee," I answered her, tickled by her question. "It's pretty awesome to see how big our world really is."

"And what a mystery the world is—what a wonderful mystery with so much to explore," Annie echoed. She glanced at me and smiled. It had been a good day for all of us.

"What was your favourite part of the tour Cole?" I asked my son.

He scrunched up his freckled face and thought for a moment. Then he jumped up with excitement. "Oh, I loved it the best when the helicopter swooped down into the valley. I felt like an eagle. That was so cool."

"Maybe you'll grow up to be a pilot one day," Annie said reaching out and smoothing back his hair. "Wouldn't that be fun." Annie had always encouraged the kids to follow their dreams. I always loved that. She always encouraged Cole and Sidnee.

ꞮG late, and the kids were yawning
ht you two it's time for bed," Annie
ᵥ ve got a big day tomorrow."
ᵤₐ tickets to see the Terry Fator show at the
ₐge. Fator is an impressionist, comedian, singer
and ventriloquist from Dallas, Texas who appeared
on America's Got Talent and won the million-dollar
prize in 2007. After that he landed a contract to
perform at The Mirage. Fator's popular show is a
great night out for families who are vacationing in
Vegas. The kids were really looking forward to it.

"You know what?" I said, as Annie and I were
cleaning up. "I feel like stretching my legs a bit.
Think I'm gonna head down to the casino and play
some roulette. Are you okay here with the kids?

She hesitated a moment and then her lips quirked
up in a slight smile. "Sure, have fun."

I had a thousand dollars' worth of chips in my
pocket and a hankering to unwind. It had been a fun
week, but I was feeling a little on edge. I hadn't had a
drop of booze in about ten days, but I told myself that
I was only going to gamble a little. Just pass the time
and then go back upstairs by 11:00 p.m. No problem,
right?

The elevators opened up onto the casino floor. I
stepped out and was immediately drawn to the
excitement surrounding me. Flashing lights and
blaring sirens and clanking coins rows of slot
machines and beyond that clusters of people shouting
out their bets. I strolled along the carpeted floor,
making my way to a roulette table. I found an empty
stool and took out a few chips, placed a ten-dollar bet
on Black 22. The wheel started spinning and when it
stopped, I won. I placed another bet and won again.

The table was buzzing with excitement. Servers were constantly coming and going bringing drinks to the other gamblers. Whisky, beer, wine, cocktails. You name it. It seemed like everyone was drinking and having a great time. So, what could it hurt? Just one drink?

In less than an hour I'd turned my 1,000 dollars into 3,800 dollars. Why not celebrate a little? Then I'd go back upstairs and surprise Annie.

There was no stopping me. I ordered a Jack Daniels and Coke and kept playing. One Jack and Coke turned into another, and then I began ordering double Jacks. "Keep them coming," I told the waiter. I placed another bet. Black 22 again. The wheel started spinning and spinning and pretty soon it felt like the whole room was spinning. Finally, the wheel stopped. I lost. I bet again and lost again. My pile of chips began to shrink as my double Jacks increased. I kept playing and drinking and losing, until I had lost my winnings, and still I kept on until I ended up losing the 1,000 dollars.

I was twelve years old when I got drunk for the first time. Mum and I were visiting my *marraine* (godmother) Louise and her son Rodney in Port Elgin. They were living in a trailer at the time, on the outskirts of town.

"Let's go for a bike ride," Rodney suggested. Rodney had his older brother's bike as well as his own.

"Sure," I replied. We hopped on the bikes and raced down the road, to a nearby park. It was early afternoon and the sun warmed our backs as we leaned our bikes against a tree and plopped down on the grass under the shade.

"Look what I got," Rodney said, pulling out a bottle.

"Canadian Club," I said reading the label.

"Wanna try?"

"I guess." I hadn't thought much about drinking up until then. I'd only had a sip of beer once or twice; it was something grown-ups did, so I didn't really care about it.

Rodney untwisted the cap and took a swig then he handed the bottle to me. I tipped it up and took a sip. Boy did it burn going down. I coughed and sputtered. Rodney laughed and slapped me on the back. He seemed to know what he was doing so I figured he had done it before.

"It's good right?" he asked with a grin.

"It tastes funny," I said, taking another tentative sip.

"Who cares how it tastes," he said. "It's how it makes you feel that counts."

"How does it make you feel?" I asked passing the bottle back to him.

"Like you're flying."

We finished the entire bottle, but I didn't feel like flying. I felt like throwing up. I vowed never to drink that stuff again. I wouldn't take another drink for a couple of years, but then when I became a teenager, it all changed, and I began to drink regularly. By the time I'd reached my 40s I'd become a functioning alcoholic.

It was four a.m. when I stumbled back to our suite. I'd lost everything and I'd gotten so drunk it was a wonder I'd even found my way back. I ended up on the couch and must have zonked out. When I woke up, bright sunlight was streaming in through the window. I groaned as I clutched my head and eased onto my back. My head hurt. My mouth felt like it was stuffed with cotton. I cracked open my eyes and the room started spinning. I closed them again and groaned. Gritting my teeth, I sat up. I managed to stand and make my way to the bedroom.

I flopped onto the bed, landing on my bloated belly.

"It's almost eight in the morning. Where were you all night?" Annie's voice echoed around the room.

She'd just walked out of the bathroom wearing a fluffy white robe, her blonde hair covered in a thick towel, turban style. "What happened to you?"

My head was pounding like a drum in a heavy metal band, so I could only groan in reply.

"You were out all night," she accused.

"Four," I rasped. "Slept on the couch."

"Four?" she replied. "That qualifies as all night."

"The car service is picking us up at ten for the Terry Fator show, and you . . ." her voice had thickened, and I knew she was trying not to cry, but for the life of me, I didn't reach out to her. My eyes were closed and so was my mind and heart. I was lost but I was too drunk to know it.

I heard rummaging around, drawers opening and closing, slippered feet padding around, muffled by plush carpet. I heard the whispered voices in the other room of Cole and Sidnee and Annie as they got ready for the morning, excited voices at first and then a *shhhh* from Annie and then one of her "Daddy's still sleeping…" excuses. Not "Daddy got drunk and can't get up yet." She was covering for me, and all I could do was lie there and let down my family. I didn't get up to greet my kids and spend time with them before the show. Instead, I fell asleep again.

Two hours later we were in the car on our way to the show. Annie and the kids were sitting in the back seat. I was sitting in the front next to the driver. I felt like shit and I must have looked it too. Cole and Sidnee chatted quietly with Annie in the back seat. It seemed like we'd been driving forever when suddenly, the driver took a sharp corner and I lost it. A gurgling and churning in my bloated belly surged up. I had to act fast. "Pull over!" I ground out.

"What's wrong?" Annie asked.

"Pull over." I couldn't say more than that. It was all I could do to hold on.

The driver pulled into an empty parking lot. The car had barely come to a halt before I opened the passenger door, leaned out, and barfed my guts out. It splashed onto the painted white concrete of the parking lot. I heaved until there was nothing left but mucus and bile. My body shivered as I flopped back in my seat, bits of my own puke peppering my shirt. The acrid stench of vomit permeated the car.

"Mummy, is Daddy sick?" Sidnee whispered from the back seat.

"Did Daddy drink again?" Cole asked. "Is he gonna be okay?"

"Daddy is fine," Annie said in a reassuring tone.

My back was to them, but I knew she had her arms around them. I knew she was trying to protect them from witnessing me go through the aftermath of yet another drinking binge.

"This is getting really old, Mr. Richardson. And I'm getting really tired," Annie said. She sounded numb, not angry. Like she had resigned herself to the inevitable—that I was never going to change. That scared the hell out of me.

"Can you just chill?" I managed as I wiped at my shirt front.

That's all I could say. I didn't have the energy to say anything else. I was in denial. I thought I could make it through the week with no drinking. Boy, was I wrong. I let down Annie, I let down the kids, and I let down myself.

Our last day in Vegas was meant to be fun, but it was miserable because of me.

I ruined everything. I ruined the entire vacation because of my drinking binge.

At the time, I couldn't see the problem. My mind was so clouded by own excuses for what I had done, that I failed to see the dangerous territory I was in.

Everything was at stake. My marriage, the respect of my children, my health. Everything.

But I was still out of control. I wasn't taking responsibility for my actions. Instead, I was giving myself permission to be self-destructive.

Have you ever been in a state like that? Where your actions threaten to erode the trust of the people who love you the most?

I was skating on thin ice, and I had no idea that the ice was about to crack.

Introduction

I Am You.

"Some people want it to happen, some wish it would happen, others make it happen."
— Michael Jordan

I am you.

I'm a just a regular person who came up through the school of hard knocks. I grew up in a small town in New Brunswick. Working class poor. I worked hard and achieved career and financial success, but at a great cost to my health and well-being, and a heavy emotional burden on my family. Why? Because of who I had become. Bitter, angry, and lost on the inside. Obese, chain-smoking, and a functioning alcoholic on the outside.

This is the story of how I changed my life.

Lessons that helped me take control of my life.

If I can do it, you can too.

You know that feeling in the pit of your stomach that never seems to go away? It's not from the double pepperoni pizza you had for lunch (although that could be part of it). It's not from that fourth cup of coffee you guzzled down to get through your afternoon meetings (although it's certainly not getting along with the pizza churning in your gut). And it's not that third cigarette you bummed off your friend in Human Resources (because the day before, you finished the last cigarette in the emergency pack you keep tucked in your bottom desk drawer).

What if you have a regular bout of panic attacks, anxiety, anger outbursts, and tension headaches? What if you keep postponing that colonoscopy because you're just too swamped at work? What if your full-package membership at that new swanky gym that opened just down the street from your house has never been used?

What if your only conversations with your son and daughter is a quick, "Hey, your lunch is on the counter. Have a good day at school." on your way out the door? What if you're so "checked-out" with your spouse that you don't even realize that they're angry with you for not getting back to them about who is going to host the family reunion this summer? What if you worry that your kids are ashamed or embarrassed of you? What if you constantly worry that your spouse is going to leave you?

Everything in your life seems off kilter. Every problem is a potential nightmare. Whether you're just coasting from day to day, or you feel so completely out of control you have to run to the washroom to either have a panic attack or throw up—or both, you've reached a point where you need to change. Not just take a sick day change. I mean REALLY change.

Completely change.

I once had the same questions running through my head as you have running through yours now: *How did I get here? And how can I make this stop?* I understand what you're going through because I was on that same hamster wheel for many years. Most of my adult life. And then I hit rock bottom, and there was nowhere else to go. I had to get up. I had to change.

In this book, I'm going to tell you what I did, and I'm going to share with you how I got here. But first, a truth.

Are you ready?

Here it is: All you have to do is one simple thing.

Own your shit.

It's not complicated science.

You don't have to buy into any super—expensive program or attend a swanky retreat.

It's something you can do for yourself and by yourself, for free.

But there's a catch: you have to do it every day.

In order to own your shit, you have to make a decision. But not just any decision. You have to make a BIG decision: the decision to change. You have to decide that every decision you make from this point on is a decision you will stick to.

So why this book? Why am I putting my life and my story out there? Why am I exposing myself this way? Let's get this straight from the get-go. I am not doing this for the money. I have a great career as a regional director in the financial services industry, I love what I do, and I love the people I work with. I have more than enough acorns squirreled away for my retirement and to take care of my family should I meet an early "hasta la vista," even though my wonderful wife Annie is a successful realtor and my kids (Cole, 21, and Sidnee, 19) are both super smart and hardworking.

I'm not worried about them; they're awesome, and they'll be fine. But I am worried about you. I want you to be fine too. I want you to feel awesome about your life, and who you are, and your place in the world.

So no, I'm not doing this for myself or my family. I am doing this because I want to help other people who are just like I was. People who have lost their way and their sense of balance in life. People who need a little help from a friend they've never met.

It's taken me many years to get to where I am today. I am not referring specifically to financial success. I am talking about "inner balance." My journey back to that balance started in 2012, but the origins of what brought me to the point of great change in my life are rooted in my childhood and youth.

There were so many life lessons that I didn't pay attention to, or that I misinterpreted because, when they happened, I was a kid and didn't know what they meant. Those moments had a huge impact on me at the time and affected my life for many years to come, but I needed to put them in perspective. I needed to reinterpret them in order to reassess my life today. I needed to understand what they truly meant back then, and how they impacted me. I'll be sharing some of those stories with you throughout this book as life lessons I've learned on my journey to Own My Shit.

My purpose in writing this book is to offer you a shortcut of sorts; to help you on your own journey to finding more balance in your life. And to help you let go of that anxiety. Balance, inner peace, happiness… call it whatever you want, but at the end of the day, the meaning behind all of it is the same: I want to help you OWN YOUR SHIT.

Owning Your Shit requires awareness, acceptance, and everyday application.

When you don't Own Your Shit, you are unaware, unhappy, and unfulfilled.

This is why every diet I tried failed. It's why I could never quit smoking for longer than a few weeks. It's why I was generally unhealthy and in terrible shape. It's why my relationship with my wife was rocky at best, and why I wasn't the father that my kids deserved. It was the reason I walked around with a grey storm cloud forever hovering over my head.

Eight years ago, I finally figured it out. It wasn't one of those *eureka* moments. It wasn't a list of many *aha* moments either. It was a slow realization that I had lost my way. My inherent values had become so buried deep inside that I didn't know how to live my life.

For all intents and purposes, at least materially, I looked like I had it all going for me. I had lots of money, a successful career, a wife and kids, and everyone was doing well—on the surface. But boy, was I skating on thin ice. You'll understand why later on.

I realized I had to go back to my childhood, figuratively, and think about my family and friends, how I grew up, and where I grew up. I had to remember. I had to remember what I had learned growing up as a working-class kid in Middle Sackville, New Brunswick back in the 1970s and 1980s.

I had to think back and remember everything my mentors taught me. I don't mean work mentors. I mean life mentors. When I was a kid and an upstart, cocky, teenager, I didn't know what a mentor was. But there were people in my life, adults, who taught me important lessons not by telling, but by showing. By how they lived and acted and treated those around them.

So, I went "back to school" in my head. I had to relearn the life lessons that had been there all along. The life lessons that I'd absorbed but didn't fully comprehend, because I'd been chasing the wrong dream instead of living the right one.

I needed to identify, clarify, and classify those lessons, and to rectify my mistakes in order to live up to who I truly wanted to be instead of who I thought I needed to be. I had to begin to piece together those life lessons and reinterpret and understand them through new eyes, because those life lessons would define my values for the rest of my life.

It took me a couple of years to do the work and figure out how to realign my goals with my values. In other words, to start Owning My Shit.

I've been Owning My Shit for almost ten years, now, and I have never been happier and healthier. I am living a balanced life. Over the past eight years, there have been lots of ups and downs, and I've been through many changes. I can now say that I've never been happier or felt more balanced in all the important areas of my life, but I also know that by no means am I perfect. And I don't want you to get the misguided notion into your head that *you* are, either.

Owning Your Shit doesn't mean being "perfect." It doesn't mean eating all your Brussels sprouts and saying no to banana cream pie. It doesn't mean doing 100 squats by 5:00 a.m. and being in your office by 6:55 or bed by 8:59 p.m. It doesn't mean turning your life into a rigid schedule where every minute is accounted for.

Owning Your Shit means taking responsibility for

the bad stuff that has brought you to this point in your life. It means making that important decision to change. It means making a commitment to that change on a daily basis. And if you slip and fall, it means getting back up again.

1. *Take responsibility for your life.*
2. *Make the decision to change.*
3. *Make a daily commitment to carry out that change.*
4. *If you slip up, admit it and get going again.*

This is my outlook in a nutshell. This is what **Own Your Shit** means at its core. This is how I live my life today and how I will keep living tomorrow, and the next day, and the day after that. If I don't **Own My Shit** every single day, then I will go back to being unaware, unhappy, and unfulfilled.

In this book, I'm going to share with you some stories from my childhood and then I'll end with a set of principles that I follow each and every day. I call them the **Own Your Shit Rules**. These principles helped guide me when I first started Owning My Shit, and they continue to guide me now.

Owning Your Shit can be applied to four key areas of our lives, what I call the **Four Foundations of Owning Your Shit.**

1. *Health/Wellness*
2. *Relationships*
3. *Money/Career*
4. *Spirituality*

I realized that in order to achieve balance in my life, I had to Own My Shit in these four areas. I was doing very well in Money/Career, but I was lacking—

big time—in the other foundations. I was moving up the corporate ladder, but there were many other factors in my life that had me out of balance. I know many of you can relate when I tell you that I was about seventy pounds overweight, ate a lot of fast food, fat food, and sugar. I was a heavy smoker and drinker. I worked long hours and never made time for exercise or my family. And finally, I was adrift when it came to a spiritual outlook.

I was in a very dark place, and I had no idea how I got there. I had to figure it all out and then put myself on the right path. It didn't happen overnight, and there were plenty of bumps and bruises along the way, but I can tell you right now that I don't have any regrets about how far I've come and the path I am on now.

This is what I want for you. I want to help as many people as I can who are stumbling or lost, or who are about to throw their hands in the air and give up. I'm here to tell you, don't give up!

You can make this happen.

You can change.

If I can do it, you can do it.

Okay, I know you've read or heard those words a gazillion times before. But there *is* truth in them. There are thousands of people out there just like me—people who had multiple problems in multiple areas of their lives, and they still changed. You can, too.

Because the one common thread in all of the problems in your life is YOU. And the solution is also YOU.

So... are you with me? Are you ready to *Own Your Shit?*

Let's do this.

Chapter 1

Make a Decision to Make a Decision.

"Sometime the questions are complicated, and the answers are simple."
—Dr Seuss

I blew out a breath and watched the billowing puffs of air float from my mouth as I stepped onto the frozen pond. A gust of wind nudged me along like an old friend, whispering in my ear, "Go fast."

I pressed the blades of my skates down on the ice and propelled myself forward. My stick scraped along the scarred surface, shifting the puck back and forth as I approached the net. A few feet away, I swung the stick back and thwacked the puck as hard I could.

WHOOSH!

The puck spiraled in an arc and landed in the net.

"He shoots! He scores!"

I hefted my stick in the air and pumped my arms as I skated a victory lap.

When I was a kid growing up in Sackville, New Brunswick, every single day I would head down to Morice's Mill Pond off Walker Road near my house.

The cows would graze on the tall, thick grass and drink from the cool water in the spring, summer, and fall, but in the winter, that pond was my playground. Or rather, my training ground. That pond was where I learned to play hockey. More importantly, it was where my dream was born.

The frozen surface of that pond in the winter was my looking glass into the future. It was where I could imagine a glimpse of how my life might be if I could get out of that small town. It was the beginning of my dream to make it to the NHL.

Dreams are wonderful to have. They can inspire us, motivate us, and help us shape our goals. When a kid dreams of becoming a pro athlete, there are three factors that have to exist: talent, commitment, and support.

As a kid, I didn't fully comprehend those factors at an intellectual level, but I did on an emotional level. I was a good player. I played in our local division in my age group, and I was good. I practiced every day and that made me better than the other boys on the team. They loved hockey, but they certainly weren't practicing every winter's day on a frozen pond, skating and shooting the puck until it was time for dinner.

They just wanted to have fun. For me, it was more than having fun. Every day after school I would go home, dump my school bag, and grab my skates from the shed behind our house. I would trudge across the field, shivering in my patched up, oversized coat. Slogging through the high snow drifts in my oversized boots that leaked after a pelting of freezing rain.

Every stitch of clothing I had on, right down to

my skates, my oversized winter coat and soggy boots, was a hand me downs from my older brothers and sisters. The kids in my family were divided into two groups of three. The first group consisted of Frances, Greg, and Cathy, separated by two years each; and the second group of us siblings came along ten years later. I was in the second group, made up of Kevin, me, and Rob. Two years separated each of us as well.

I wouldn't know what it meant to own something new until I started working and making money. Back then, money, or my family's lack thereof, was a driving force for me in my quest to make it to the NHL. I dreamed of becoming someone. Of making my parents proud. Of being that small-town kid who "made it out" and became someone big and famous.

By the time I got to the pond, I was usually almost as frozen as the water itself, and my feet were damp. But that didn't deter me because I knew once I laced up and stepped onto the icy surface, my teeth would stop chattering. As I glided from one end of the ice to the other, shifting the puck back and forth with my stick, I was no longer at Morice's Mill Pond in Middle Sackville… I was soaring.

A frozen pond was where I learned to play hockey. It was also where I learned to dream.

Hockey wasn't just about having fun for me. There was something inside me that made me yearn for something more. At the time, I didn't know what it was. I thought my dream meant playing in the NHL. I thought that would be it. That was want I wanted. I was so sure back then as a kid of nine years old that making it to the NHL would be the answer to everything. It would be a dream come true.

It would be decades before I fully realized what

my dream was truly about—and what happiness meant.

I'm of the firm belief that one of the greatest pleasures in life is taking your kids to hockey games. My son is a talented hockey player, and isn't it one of the great Canadian dreams to play in the NHL or the WHL? Or to play on Canada's National Olympic Team?

In 2012, I took my then, 14-year-old son, Cole, to a hockey game.

It was the World Junior Ice Hockey Championships, and Canada was going head to head against the Russians at the Saddledome in Calgary. The arena was packed with more than 19,000 fans, give or take. Now, I can't think of any Canadian who doesn't love hockey—no matter where you live in Canada, no matter what your ethnicity, and no matter where you or your family originally came from, hockey is Canada's game.

Even folks who aren't *hardcore* fans tune into the game every time Canada steps on the ice to play Russia. Given that I have loved the game my entire life and aspired to play pro, and given that my son played hockey from a wee age and aspired to play pro, we didn't just watch the game, we *experienced* it. Analyzing every play, counting the shots on goal, and basically coaching from the sidelines. Yup. Hockey geek right here.

When I took Cole to the World Junior game that night—January 3, 2012—I was so far away from Owning My Shit that I wouldn't have recognized it if I'd stepped in it. But that night was the beginning of a shift for me. It put me on the path to Owning My Shit, and it will be forever seared in my memory. I was 44 years old, and I was about to learn the most valuable lesson of my life.

I plunked myself down beside Cole, loaded down with two oversized slices of pepperoni pizza, nacho chips with gooey melted cheese, and two mega cups of drinks. An orange drink for Cole and a beer for me. You can't enjoy a game without some nosh, right? We were sitting a few rows up from centre ice, so we had a clear view of the puck action, and we could hear the coaches on the Canadian side. The game was a nail-biter, Canada and Russia were well matched. Tough.

Feeling restless, I chugged down my beer and then got up for another. Hockey games can go on for a long time, especially with all stops due to penalties, fights, and injuries. As I made my way back down the steps to our seat, I spied Cole's blond head, he'd just taken off his toque. I swallowed a lump in my throat as I sat back down. My son. I was so proud of him. He was such a good kid. Smart, talented, and a far better hockey player than I ever was.

"Having a good time, son?"

"Yeah, Dad. I hope we win."

"Well, we learn from the losses just as much as we learn from the wins, Cole."

"Yeah, Coach tells us that too."

"Did I ever tell you that when I was a kid, everyone was convinced I'd end up playing for the NHL?"

My son glanced at me and nodded. "Yeah, Dad you told me." He smiled that goofy smile that kids get when they indulge their parents' childhood stories.

I reached out and mussed his hair. "Well, never

give up on your dreams, Cole, even if they take you on a different road."

"Are you sad you never ended up playing?"

"Nah." I shrugged and took a long sip of my beer. "It wasn't meant to be." That was the truth, wasn't it? It wasn't meant to be. I was good enough for Middle Sackville but not for Calgary.

Not good enough.

How do you let go of a broken dream? How do you come to terms with the loss of the biggest passion you had as a kid? The dream that sustained you through a very tough childhood?

I took another sip and turned back to the action on the ice, my eye following the gliding skates, the stick shifting the puck back and forth as the Canadian player approached the net. He pulled back his stick, thwacked the puck, and shot it in.

He shoots, he scores!

In my mind, I was back home, skating on that frozen pond, gliding on the scarred surface of the ice, my own stick shifting the puck and forth. My passion flowing through my veins. My dream of playing in the NHL driving me forward.

What happened to that kid?

Why did he end up like me?

Oh, I was successful by all accounts. I made a great living in the financial planning world. I provided well for my family. Big house, two nice cars, vacations to Mexico. But the passion of the kid I'd been was gone. The inner light that made me dream for something big...

It was gone.

I wished I could get it back.

I glanced at Cole, who intently watched the game.

If my son wanted to play for the NHL, I would support him with every fibre of my being. He was a talented player—way more talented than I was at his age. But even if he chose not to pursue hockey, Cole was smart, kind, and a team player. He would have no problems finding his path.

So why was I so dissatisfied? What was wrong with me?

I took another sip of beer, thinking that I was just a silly, middle-aged man, pondering what never was.

What I didn't know was that I was about to go through something life changing that would force me to truly examine my life and my own path.

As for the game, Russia beat Canada 6-5, but I can't blame what happened that night on Canada losing the game. Nope. There was something churning inside of me that night, and instead of thinking about it, I decided to drink it away. I forget how much beer I drank. After all, I was having a good time with my son. Nothing new there. I'd been chugging beer in front of my son his entire life, so I didn't think anything of it. I didn't expect him to think anything of it either.

Looking back now, I can't help but think about all those times I drank in front of my son and daughter at a family Christmas party or Thanksgiving or watching a hockey game. I'm not talking about one glass of wine with dinner. I'm talking about three, four, five beers. How did my kids feel about my drinking? Were they worried that I drank too much? Were they ashamed that their dad got a little too loud and a little too argumentative at beer number four?

The night of January 3, 2012, as Canada was going up against Russia, did my son worry that I would get so drunk that I would stumble down the stairs in our section, or pick a fight with the guy who bumped into me as the spectators were elbow-to-elbow exiting the arena? I don't know the answer to that because I was *behaving* like a shit, but I wasn't *owning* my shit. It was bad enough that I got drunk in front of my son, it was worse that I had no idea the impact it had on him. Some of you might not care about that, or you may have never considered the full ramifications of drinking in front of your kids. After all, what's wrong with throwing back a few, right? Wrong. My son was underage, so my behaviour wasn't exactly on the Top Ten best parent moves in the parenting handbook.

That night, I didn't think about the impact that my drinking was having on my son. I didn't think about the possibility of my son feeling anxiety as he watched me drain cup after cup of beer. It never occurred to me that my son might have been watching my flushed face or hearing my too loud voice and slurred words. It never occurred to me that my son might have been nervously watching my movements, worried that something might happen.

No. I wasn't aware of any of that. I was too focussed on "having a good time" and "getting into the game" to notice how my drinking was affecting my teenage son.

After the game, we got up and made our way up the aisle out to the landing. Better to use the stairs rather than try for the elevator. It was slow going because of the crowds. As we neared the top of the bleachers I stumbled and reached for the seat on my right to break my fall.

"Dad!" Cole grabbed my arm to steady me.

"Thanks s-s-on." I put my hand on Cole's shoulder. I told myself it was because I didn't want to lose him in the crowd, but I saw the concern in his eyes.

You're getting old, Timmy.

I was overheated, but I told myself that it was because it was hot in the arena. When we got outside, I took a deep breath of fresh air. It wasn't cold, but compared to the stuffy arena, it was a welcome relief. My head felt a bit clearer.

Not clear enough, though.

As we walked to the parking lot, I couldn't help but think about the kid I used to be. Was he still inside me? Why had I forgotten about him?

In truth, I was the furthest away from self-awareness that I have ever been in my life. Maybe I was feeling nostalgic. Maybe I was just feeling sorry for myself that night.

What do you have to be sorry about, Tim Richardson?

As we approached our car in the parking lot, I noticed an SUV blocking us in. It was Annie.

"What are you doing here?" I asked after she rolled down the window.

"I'm here to drive you guys home," she replied in a stiff tone.

"Why?" I asked, confused. "I drove us here."

"I texted Mom," Cole said in a quiet voice.

I turned to Cole. "You wanted Mom to—" I scrubbed my hands down my face. Yes, I'd consumed several beers during the game, but . . .

"Dad, you almost fell."

What I saw in his eyes broke my heart.

He looked nervous, worried, scared—and maybe even ashamed.

I patted Cole on the shoulder. "Okay, son, Mom will drive you home and I'll drive my car.

"Dad no!" Cole pleaded. "Come with us."

"Tim, get in the car," Annie said bluntly.

I turned back to her and saw the anger flash in her eyes. And something else. Disgust.

"Leave your car," she went on. "We'll call the arena security to let them know, and we'll call for a tow-truck."

"No." I was adamant. "I'll drive myself home." I was acting like an idiot, but I just couldn't get into the SUV. Annie was pissed off at me. Again. And Cole was worried and ashamed of his own father.

"You're drunk," she shot back.

"I'm fine. I've driven home like this plenty of times." I was in full-blown idiot mode now.

Annie shook her head as she stared out the windshield. "Fine," she said, not sparing me a second glance. "We'll follow you. Just take it slow, okay?"

"I know how to drive," I snapped, not caring that people were watching us as they made their way to their cars. But Annie cared. Cole cared. They saw what I refused to see. Annie reversed and gave me space to pull out of the parking spot. Then we made our way out of the lot and drove home.

"Tim, you fuckin' did it again," I said slapping the wheel. I should have just had Annie drive us and pick us up. I would have still gotten drunk, but at least we could have avoided the entire mess in the parking lot. Hell, I hadn't even realized the risk I had been about to make, if not for the maturity of my son. I kept my window rolled down so the cold air would help me stay clearheaded.

Drunk driving is a stupid thing. I think it's one of

the stupidest things that people do. Maybe this has happened to you—you're at a friend's house or a restaurant or bar, and you've had a few. You may have thought to yourself, *"Hey, I'm okay to drive. I didn't drink that much. I'm fine. Really."* We've all been there. I can't tell you the number of times I thought that myself, or the number of times I've done it. How many times have you had a few drinks and gotten behind the wheel of a vehicle? Two? Three? Five?

But the thing is, *one time is too many.*

When people talk about "being in a dark place," the phrase can sound somewhat cliché. But there is truth in those words, and I was in a very dark place. I love my wife and kids with everything in my heart, and for many years, I worked hard and provided well for them. But there was something big missing from my life.

I wasn't Owning My Shit.

I believe in telling people what's on my mind. I believe in speaking the truth. I believe in "telling it like it is." Part of that is just who I am, down to my bones. Part of that is where I come from and what I experienced growing up in Middle Sackville, NB.

Everyone around me drank. The drink of choice was usually beer, because everything else was just too expensive. Drinking was something you did with your friends on the weekends. It was something you did watching sporting events. It was something you did at family celebrations. Drinking helped me feel better, helped me get in a party mood, helped me fit in, helped me get along with others.

Drinking also made me forget. It made me forget when I was unhappy, when I was frustrated, when I was nervous, and when I was just plain angry.

But that fateful night in January, when I made the decision to drink at that hockey game, I didn't think of it as a bad decision. Heck, I didn't even stop to think at all. I didn't stop to consider how Cole would feel. I didn't stop to think about the consequences of drinking and then driving. I didn't stop to think of the consequences for my marriage and my kids.

Have you ever done something completely fucked up and you have no idea why?

That was my head space that night. I thought I was having a good time. I thought I was just out for a great night with my kid. I thought I was just having fun. That's what I told myself every time I popped the cap off a bottle or stepped up to a bar for a pint: *I'm just having fun.*

That was the furthest thing from the truth.

Because the truth was, I didn't know how to enjoy myself without that buzz. I didn't know how to interact with people in an honest, open way without the boost of a couple of beers. I didn't know how to cope with the all the bad stuff in my life without the help of booze.

It had started to snow on the drive home, but I still kept the window rolled down. I needed that frigid slap to my face. I needed to wake up. Crystalline snowflakes floated in through the open window, taking me back to my childhood again, when I learned that no two snowflakes are the same. Magic. The first snowfall that I can remember, I ran outside and gazed up at the sky. I held out my palms, hoping to catch as many snowflakes as I could. Wanting to see what each one looked like. I stuck my tongue out, wondering if each one tasted differently, too.

Now the snowflakes swirled around me in the car,

landing on my cheeks, melting with the heat of my skin. Water trickled down the weathered grooves of my face, blending with the tears that had begun to fall.

My glance strayed to the rear-view mirror. Annie was saying something to Cole. They were close enough behind me that I could see her talking. Probably asking him about the game. I knew without a doubt that Annie would never say anything bad about me to the kids. She was probably trying to keep things light. Keep Cole from asking about me. I knew her well.

I didn't realize it then, but that drive home was a turning point for me.

My son. The look in his eyes. I couldn't get it out of my head.

Annie. She was just trying to keep our son safe. Hell, she was trying to keep me safe, too. It was only my stubborn pride that made me get into my car and drive myself home.

I knew how much she loved Cole and Sidnee. She would step in front of a moving car to save them. She would take a bullet in the chest for them. She would do that for me, too. She was a protective Mama Bear.

So why did I make it so hard for her to do what she does so beautifully and naturally—love us, take care of us?

I didn't have the answer to those questions, or to the many more swirling around my head like those heavy snowflakes.

We got home safe.

But I wasn't sound.

As we got out of the car and walked into the house, Annie asked if we wanted a hot chocolate. Sidnee was at a sleepover at a friend's house.

"Nah, I think I'm going to head up to bed," I said.

"Dad, what about the marshmallows? Mom bought the big ones," Cole said in excitement. My eyes met Annie's. Ice. I decided it was best to retreat.

I ruffled Cole's hair. "I think Dad needs a hot shower and then bed."

"Okay." Cole nodded. "Good night, Dad."

"Good night, son." I gave him a quick hug and trudged upstairs. My knees wobbled like a frail old man's as I made my way to the bathroom.

I stared at myself in the mirror for a long, long time.

"What are you fucking doing?" I asked out loud. My voice sounded distant, faraway, like I was speaking against the wind, but I began hurling more questions at my reflection. "Why did you drink tonight? Why didn't you get in the car with Annie and Cole? Why are you such a fuck-up? Why do you keep drinking like this? And what about your diet? Why do you eat so much crap? Why do you smoke a pack a day? Why don't you work out? Why do you work long hours and weekends? Why do you make less and less time for Annie and Cole and Sidnee? Why do you only care about making money? Don't you give a shit about your life?"

"What *do* you give a shit about?" I shouted at the mirror.

What, indeed? What happened to that kid gliding on Morice's Mill Pond?

In that moment, I had no answers. Only questions. But I was determined to find the answers. I had taken the first step. I had become aware.

My heart pounded in my chest. My ears rang. My breath came in short, sharp gasps. I was hurtling down into a black hole like a free-falling elevator.

How many times had I done the very same thing, with or without Annie or Cole or Sidnee in the car? How many times had I put their lives in danger? How many times had I put my own life at risk?

Maybe I had been within the legal limit. Maybe I had been perfectly fine to drive. But that wasn't the point. The truth was, I was acting like an idiot. I was thinking only of myself. Hell, I wasn't even doing that. I wasn't thinking at all. The fact that I would put my son's life in peril was unforgiveable. When I think about it today, I start to shake all over again. What was I doing?

Bile rose in my throat. I gagged and took some deep breaths as I tried to calm myself. I hopped into the shower and let the hot spray wash over me. When I was done, I flicked off the light in the bathroom and walked into the bedroom. Annie was just slipping on her pajamas—white flannel decorated with pink hearts—and her strawberry blonde hair was tied up in a loose top knot. She looked sweet and vulnerable.

My guilt sat like lump in my chest as I slipped into bed and made a show of stacking up a few pillows behind my head.

Wisps of fine hair framed her pretty face. "Can we talk?" she asked. The ice had thawed a bit, but the hurt was still there. "What happened back there? You couldn't stay away from drinking for one night?"

Had she heard me yelling at myself in the bathroom?

"I—I didn't realize I drank that much—" Shit. I was just giving her another stupid excuse. I rubbed the back of my neck, knowing it was now or never. "I'm sorry. I shouldn't have had anything to drink. I should have texted you myself." I heaved a big sigh. "Cole's a smart kid."

"Yes, he is," she replied in a quiet voice. "Tell me why?"

One simple question. One simple word. I didn't have an answer for her. How could I give an answer when there was none? No justification for being that stupid, thoughtless, careless. Annie turned out the light and slipped into the bed beside me.

"Cole could have been hurt. Or worse," she whispered brokenly. "You could have killed my son. You could have killed yourself."

Her accusation sliced through me. "He's my son, too," I said thickly.

"Oh no, you don't. You don't get to feel sorry for yourself. Not after what you almost did."

"I'm sorry."

"You're sorry? How many times have you said that to me? To the kids?"

I glanced at her profile. She was staring into the darkness.

And it *was* dark. I'd brought us to this place. This abyss. This point of no return.

How many chances does your wife give you before it's the last chance? Had I used up my last chance?

How could I tell her what was in my heart, when I didn't even know how to put it into words? I was a failure. I was desperate. I had to do something change the course of where we were headed. Then it hit me like a lightning bolt. Something I used to do as a kid before every big hockey tournament: I'd go into hardcore training mode. "I'm not going to take a drink for 30 days," I blurted.

"Really?" she said sarcastically. "You think that 30 days is going to do the trick? You think that's going to change everything?" Anger laced her words. "You promised me that you wouldn't drink when we were in Vegas and then you got stinking drunk to the point where we had to stop the car so you could puke in a parking lot."

I deserved her anger. I deserved her sarcasm.

"Look, I have to do *something*," I said. "I won't touch a drop for a month. I need to show you that I can do this."

"I'll believe it when I see it." Annie turned over, her back to me. I continued to lay there, staring into the dark. I knew she didn't believe me. She didn't believe I could do it. At this point, she had lost all trust in me. Hell, I'd lost all trust in myself. I didn't deserve her trust, but I could earn it. I could earn it back, one day at a time. I could earn back the trust of my children, too, one day at a time. That's all I could do.

The day after the hockey game, I stopped by a Chapters bookstore on my lunch break and wandered around, looking for something to read. A book that could give me some answers. I found that book, and I bought it and read it from cover to cover. It resonated with me. It resonated because I was ready for it, and it has stayed with me ever since. Susan Jeffers's *Feel the Fear and Do It Anyway* made me see what I had failed to see for many years. It also made me realize that I had to make a change.

For the next month, I stopped drinking. No beer, no wine, nothing. I read the Susan Jeffers book. I began writing my thoughts down. I began to ask my questions. Why did I drink? What did I feel inside when I drank? Why did I keep breaking my promises? What had happened to me? I wrote down my answers. I filled an entire notebook—then another one. I went back to the bookstore and looked for more books to read. More insight. Was I an alcoholic? Should I go to AA?

Over the course of the 30 days, I began to make other changes. I cut out junk food and started eating better. I got back on the treadmill and tried jogging for thirty minutes. I almost had a heart attack. I called my doctor, who's also a friend of mine, and he told me to stop being an idiot. "Walk for ten minutes," he said. "Do that three times a day."

I did.

Annie thawed over the course of the month as she watched me make an effort. She'd shifted from anger, to wariness, to encouragement. The kids were excited too. They began to opt for things such as chicken salad instead of chicken fingers and fries.

At the end of the 30 days, Annie came home from her errands. She walked into the kitchen and set her bags on the counter. I was chopping onions and carrots for our stir fry.

As she put away the items Annie pulled out an expensive bottle of wine and set it on the counter. I stared at the bottle for a moment. Then I looked at her.

"To celebrate. You made it through 30 days with no drinking." She smiled.

Thirty days before, I would have said yes to celebrating with wine. Nothing wrong with that. A lot of people go on diets before a cruise because they know they'll be indulging for ten days straight. Wasn't this the same thing? A celebration of my achievement. I had done it. I hadn't had a drink in 30 days.

Annie continued to put away the items she'd bought at the store. My gaze went back to the bottle. Something had begun to shift inside me. Something I had forgotten. Something I'd had as a kid.

Drive. Perseverance. Determination.

I had managed to rekindle that flame of inner strength. That doggedness I'd had as a kid when I went after a goal. For too many years, I had numbed it with booze, smoking, and eating junk… but now I could feel that resilience growing inside me once more.

My hard work was starting to show. I was feeling better. I had more energy. More focus. My mood was better. I'd lost some of my body bloat. And that was just after 30 days. Imagine if I kept going. Kept reading. Kept writing my thoughts. Kept exercising and eating healthy.

"You know what, honey? If you don't mind, I'm going to skip the wine for our celebration. I'm going to try to keep going without the drinking."

"Are you sure?" she said.

I nodded. "Yeah, I'm sure. I'm feeling pretty good. I'm going to keep going."

She wrapped her arms around me and kissed me. "OK," she whispered. "I'm proud of you."

Those words meant more to me than anything I could say to myself. She believed in me. And more importantly, I was starting to believe in myself.

"Tell me how you're feeling inside?" she asked me.

And I did. Everything began to pour out of me. I had been worried about talking to her. I felt I needed to prove to her that I could do it, that I could stop drinking. But I proved it to myself, too. I had been reading and writing my thoughts down for the past month, and now I was ready to talk.

Annie listened to me, and for the first time in a long time, we didn't just talk, we communicated. We shared our thoughts and fears—and we took that first step toward healing.

Annie is my rock, and without her, I would not be here today. I would not have been able to make the changes in my life that I needed to make. I love her and honour her with everything that I am. My kids are my world: Cole is my hero, and Sidnee is my light. I love them and admire the young adults they have become. I hope that the changes that I made in my life have had a positive impact on them.

My purpose is to make them proud every day.

As I talked to Annie, I knew I needed to *decide*. I needed to do something different. But it couldn't be temporary. And I needed to do it every single day. I knew this change would need to impact every aspect of my life. I also knew that if I didn't make that decision to change, right then and there, I would never do it.

So, I decided. I *made a decision* to change every negative thing in my life from that day on. My goals were big. Huge, even, because I was determined to make everything better. I decided to stop drinking. Stop smoking. Lose weight. Exercise. Sleep better. Be "present" in my life. Communicate better with my family, friends, and coworkers. Be a better person. Stop using my drive for success in my job as an excuse not to take ownership of my life. Did I want to make tons of money, or did I want to make a difference?

There so many things to change. The list seemed insurmountable, and I had no idea how I would do it all. But I had made my decision, and I had committed myself. There was no way I was going back on that.

No way.

And I did figure it out—as soon as I realized that I consistently failed at doing something very important: Owning My Shit. I had never taken responsibility for the excesses in my life, overeating, drinking, smoking etc., and I had never fully committed to making positive changes in my life. I'd never stuck to them.

So, I did a complete one-eighty. It was big. It was life changing.

Over that first year of Owning My Shit, I stopped eating junk and started eating healthy food, and I made exercise a daily part of my life. As a result, I lost about 70 pounds. I quit smoking cold turkey. I quit drinking. I began to read a lot of books that helped me figure out what was going on inside me. I began to change the way I communicated with my family, friends, coworkers, and everyone I interacted with. My relationships with the people I loved most in my life, Annie, Cole, and Sidnee, were the best they'd ever been.

When I quit drinking, Cole was 14, and Sidnee was 13. One of the single most important reasons for me quitting was that I was very aware that my children were watching my every move. When I started to Own My Shit, I began to learn what it meant to be dedicated to my life and all the people in it.

I wasn't suddenly "Dad of the Year," but I began to truly listen to their concerns and problems, and to help them solve them. When you spend high quality time with your children, you create a unique bond with them.

As a parent, I fully believe that the number one gift you can give your children is self-confidence. I think it's even more important than unconditional love. As they grow up and forge their own lives, their ability to be proud of who they are and to believe in themselves is connected to you and how you believe in your life—and to how you treat yourself.

Both Cole and Sidnee were offered multiple athletic scholarships when they graduated from high school. They inspire me every day with their strength and determination, their joy in going after a goal and achieving it.

In our house we have a swear jar. Every time someone says a particular word, a loonie (one dollar) goes into that jar. You might think you know what our "bad" word is, but you would likely be wrong. The word is *can't*. We've had that swear jar for years, and boy, has it seen a lot of change. In more ways than one.

When I decided to Own My Shit, everything changed. I made a decision to make a decision. And I didn't negotiate with myself.

Now, it's your turn.

Take a good, hard look at yourself and your life. What is holding you back? Do you have someone in your life you can talk to and share with? A spouse, friend, co-worker, spiritual advisor, therapist, even a hotline? If not, then talk to yourself. Be honest. Heck, look in the mirror if you have to. Go for a walk or drive to a peaceful place in nature and just have a real, honest-to-goodness straight-shooting conversation with yourself.

Deep down, you know what's wrong. You know what's bugging you. You know what's eating you up inside. You know what's holding you back. Say it to the universe. And then take a deep breath. Seek help. Start with your family doctor. Go online and look for a psychologist based in your area. Talk to your spiritual advisor if you have one. Go to an AA or NA meeting. Talk to a friend. It's going to be all right.

How do I know this? Because I said the same thing to myself ten years ago. And guess what? It's all right.

Chapter 2

Turn Shame into Humility.

"Life is a long lesson in humility."
— *J.M. Barrie*

Please don't let it be me. Please don't let it be me. Please don't let it be me.

I will always remember those words. Like a mantra. They will forever be embedded in my mind.

I was terrified it would be me.

I was thirteen years old on that hot, sunny day in June 1980. Almost the end of another school year, it was "field day" where all the kids at Salem Elementary School took place in track and field events. Long jump, high jump, sprints, and the endurance run. It was a fun day, the kind I liked. More fun than doing math problems at my desk. The teachers had fun too. They handed out popsicles from coolers set up around the field. They even gave us lunch: plastic cups filled with a cold orange drink, and hot dogs and burgers cooked up on Hibachi grills set up in the parking lot.

In the afternoon after all the field events were completed, the school principal, Mrs. Fisher, called all the students in grades four, five, and six for an assembly in the gymnasium. We all sat clustered in little groups with our homeroom classes. The younger grades in the front, with the older grades behind. It was hot in the gym. There was no air conditioning, of course. but the doors were open to generate a cross breeze, and the teachers had plugged in several fans to help circulate the air. I sat cross-legged on the gleaming, waxed wood floor.

This was it. The moment all the kids had been waiting for. The David Sears Memorial Trophy was going to be awarded to the student with the best combined athletic and scholastic ability. Most students thought it was a foregone conclusion that my best friend, Sammy Roth, was going to be the "chosen one" that year.

Sammy, a tall, lean boy with a shock of blond hair, could run as fast as the wind. His best sport was soccer, but he excelled at every sport he tried. The gym was buzzing with excitement, and everyone was chattering about who they thought would snag the David Sears.

Sammy leaned in and whispered to me, "You're gonna win this thing, Tim." He nodded as if to confirm it.

I shrugged, attempting to look nonchalant, as if it didn't matter to me either way.

But it did matter. It mattered a lot.

My stomach was doing back flips. My ears were buzzing. My palms were damp.

On the one hand, I really wanted the trophy. I wanted to take it home, and then during dinner, when all the family was gathered, I would get up, pull it out of my back pack and set it on the kitchen table. Right in front of Mom and Dad. I wanted them to see what I had accomplished. To know that their son Timmy was good for something. That I was a winner.

But on the other hand, I was terrified to win. Yes. Terrified.

If I won, I'd have to do what I didn't want to do. I would have to stand up and walk to the podium where Mrs. Fisher and Mrs. Sears were standing. And then I'd have to turn and face everyone in the school and say something.

And everyone would see what I was wearing—my bell-bottom pants.

No one wore bell-bottoms. Except me. Back then, the punk rock look was more popular, black t-shirts and straight-legged jeans. That was the cool look everyone was after.

What did it matter? I went to school every day wearing those pants. Well, it's one thing to blend into a crowd. It's quite different to stand up *in front* of everyone and accept an award. I wasn't a rich kid. I didn't have money. What if everyone thought I was getting the award because Mrs. Fisher felt sorry for me? What if they thought I didn't deserve it? After all, Sammy was the better athlete. I didn't want anyone laughing at me. Or whispering and pointing at me. Or talking behind my back. I clenched my fists in my lap, scrunched my eyes tight, and prayed that I wouldn't get the trophy.

Please don't let it be me. Please don't let it be me. Please don't let it be me.

I prayed so hard, that sweat beaded on my forehead. I started breathing in short, sharp gasps. I'd spent the past five years as an altar boy at Holy Rosary Church and St. Vincent Church. I figured I had logged enough hours that God would surely listen to me.

"And the David Sears Trophy goes to…"

Please God, let Sammy win the award and I will do the 9:00 and the 11:00 mass for the next three months at both locations. Please, don't make me win. Don't make me have to get up in from the whole school wearing these pants…

"… Tim Richardson!"

And there I was, on the front page of the local section of *The Sackville Tribune* for all eternity. The picture showing a teary-eyed Norma Sears handing me the trophy named after her beloved son, David, who'd passed away a few years before.

I looked like I was about to start crying too.

The congratulations and well wishes followed me everywhere for the next few days from friends and teachers. Many people made a point of commenting on how emotional I was at the assembly.

"You must have known David Sears really well," an older teacher smiled and patted me on the back.

"I knew him a little bit," I replied, ducking my head bashfully.

But the truth was, I didn't know David Sears. In fact, I'd never met him. Why did I lie? Was it so I wouldn't hurt the teacher's feelings? Or was it because I didn't want anyone to know that I had been so worried about standing in front of the entire school wearing my bell-bottom pants, that it was all I could do to hold back my own tears?

It wasn't a bad lie. It was more like a little white lie. No one got hurt because of it. In fact, when I told the teacher that I knew him a little, she beamed at me. Her eyes glistened as though *she* was trying not to cry. My lie made an old lady happy. It made her believe in the goodness of humanity. That even though David Sears had died, his friend, Timmy Richardson, was carrying the torch for him. David Sears would live on in the accomplishments of Timmy Richardson.

At the time, I had all sorts of excuses spinning around in my head about my lie. But the truth was, I had lied because it was easier than telling the truth. The truth was raw. The truth was painful. The truth was about my shame. About my feeling not good enough because of my hand-me-down clothes. Because everyone could see that I was poor.

When I accepted the award and turned to look out at the entire school assembly, they clapped and cheered. They didn't jeer. They didn't point and laugh at me. Sure, there were a few kids who must have snickered at my pants. But almost everyone was happy for me. I was given a special award for excelling in athletics and academics. I was good at both. Maybe Sammy Roth was a better athlete, but the David Sears trophy was about overall achievement.

I had won a beautiful award that honored the life of a boy taken from this earth far too soon, but I didn't appreciate the truth of that. Instead, I told a lie about knowing David Sears. I wish I had known him. I wish I had met him. Maybe we could have been friends. But telling a lie, telling everyone that I knew him when I didn't—well, that somehow tarnished the meaning of the award. I'd let the Sears family down, and I dishonored David's memory by pretending I had known him.

I was all of thirteen years old, but it wasn't my

age that mattered. I was old enough to know better. I should have known better. But I allowed my shame to take over and make me feel unworthy, simply because of the pants I wore.

It would be many years before I learned the true lesson of that day or the true meaning of that trophy. Many years before I understood the great honour that I was given, in the name of David Sears, a boy who died so tragically and so young.

The David Sears Trophy was not meant to show that I was better than all the other kids or to reward me for being the best all-around student and athlete in the school. It wasn't meant to reward the best dressed kid in the school, either. It certainly didn't change the way I thought about myself. I lied about knowing David Sears, so I clearly didn't understand the meaning of that honour. No, the David Sears Trophy represented the potential we all have inside us to be better people, to strive for our goals, to work hard for what's important in life, and to understand that achievement is not based on how we look but what we can accomplish.

As I got older, started working, and established a successful career, I began to accumulate the kind of wardrobe that I could never have even fathomed back in those bell-bottom days. Designer shirts, bespoke tailored suits, silk ties. No more hand-me downs—only the best for me. You could say that I became something of a clotheshorse. If "clothes make the man," I *was* the man. My clothes made me able to project a confidence I didn't have when I was a kid, but under that projected confidence, I still lacked self-esteem.

Today, many years later, I know the difference

between confidence and self-esteem. Confidence is what we project. Self-esteem is who we are.

Ah, but when I was in my 20s and 30s, when I was "the man" on the outside, I was still that kid in hand-me-down bell-bottom pants on the inside. In fact, ever since that moment in the school gymnasium, every time I had to give a speech or presentation, I went back to praying, "Please don't let it be me." Because underneath all my so-called confidence, I was still the kid who just wanted to run away and hide.

Clothes became my disguise. Clothes became my armour. I didn't have true self-esteem, so I used a fancy wardrobe to project a confident avatar. I was the guy who *looked* like he had his shit together instead of being the guy who *Owned* His Shit. My clothes did the talking for me. They told everyone that I was successful. That I had "arrived." That I had money. That I had achieved something. That I was worthy.

It took years of deep self-reflection to understand what I was and what I had done for so many years. And it took a lot soul searching to understand what was going on inside the mind and heart of that the kid in the bell-bottom pants who became the guy with a walk-in closet full of fancy duds.

When I began my inward journey in 2012, I had to figure out the difference between projected confidence and true self-esteem, including examining my reasons for dressing the way I did. That didn't mean I suddenly started wearing torn jeans to work. No, of course not. I still had to dress like a professional. I do believe that proper business attire is appropriate in the workplace. While many companies incorporate a "jeans Friday" or a relaxed dress code, I'm still the guy in the pressed trousers, cuffed shirt, and tie. And while there are many fashion-hip people who love shopping in thrift stores and vintage clothing shops, searching for the very same kind of bell-bottom pants that I used to wear as a kid, I continue to visit a talented tailor in Montreal who makes my suits.

But today, I wear the nice clothes, they don't wear me. My clothes are no longer a burden that I carry. They are no longer a disguise hiding the insecure kid in threadbare, bell-bottom pants. Quite simply, I feel good inside, and my clothes reflect that.

Today, when I step in front of a room full of people, I no longer feel a desperate need to project confidence. I carry myself with dignity and humility. That means I don't let my ego get in the way of communicating, connecting, and collaborating with people.

Today, I am no longer the guy who looks like he has his act together. There is no act. I am the guy who Owns His Shit every day.

More than forty years have passed since that fateful day when I was awarded the David Sears Trophy but didn't understand its significance. It took me decades to appreciate the life lesson I learned that day. I am honoured and humbled that my school and the Sears family awarded me the that trophy, and I will do my best to live up to that honour. If I could speak to David Sears today, I would say two simple words: "Thank you."

When you look back at your childhood, what was a moment (or moments) that you regret? If you could have a "do-over," what would you have said or done differently?

Open your lap top or grab a pen and paper (or a journal), and jot down what you would have changed, if you could. Think about the little kid you were. What would you say to that kid if you could talk to them? Now, give that kid a hug, because it's going to be okay. And remember... never forget that kid.

Chapter 3

Don't Forget Where You Came From, But Don't Let It Keep You from Where You're Going.

"When you finally go back to your old hometown, you find it wasn't the old home you missed but your childhood."
—Sam Ewing

Remember that first time when you were able to remember your home address? Wasn't that a big moment in your little-kid life? A proud moment? You knew the number of your house and the street where you lived. You recited it out loud to your parents over and over again. Maybe they smiled indulgently at the lisp in your voice as you tried to wrap your tongue around the new sounds.

I never had that moment. My house didn't have a number so there was nothing to memorize. Numbers became important to me. Numbers represented many things in my life. The number of dimes I needed to buy a chocolate bar. The number of laps I had to skate around Morice's Mill Pond before I would allow myself to end my practice. The number of times Mum patched up my pants. My age when I realized just how poor my family was.

It's ironic that I ended up in a line of work that had to do with numbers. But while numbers might be the backbone of my work, people are the heart and soul.

As I mentioned earlier, I work in the wealth management industry. I began as a financial planner when I was 27 years old and I have worked very hard over the years. I managed the most profitable team in Calgary. We were profitable not because we were chasing after dollars, however, but because we worked together as a team to offer the best services we could to our families. Yes, our families. Not just clients. We work with *families*, helping them manage the most important aspects of their lives—marriage, births, education, homes, accidents, health issues, retirement, funerals, and everything in between.

Because it's not about business, it's about people.

And I don't have employees; I work with my team.

Leadership is about learning. Every single day.

How does a kid who grew up in a house with no number in Middle Sackville, New Brunswick get to where I am today? Numbers and people. Numbers and emotions. As a kid, I was ashamed that my house had no number. I was ashamed that I lived in a rundown old nun's house. I was ashamed that when I had to write my address down on any official school document, I could only write Walker Road.

The old nun's house down the street from the Holy Rosary Church.

A square, two-storey, wood framed house with a shed in back. Aluminum siding eventually replaced the chipped white-painted wood on most of the house, but one section remained bare except for a tarp that had been hammered in place with a few rusty nails. The front porch was falling off the house, and on winter days after a snowfall, we had to shovel our way off that porch in order to make our way to school.

Dad had cut out part of the wall to insert another window for more light and air circulation, but he never got around to finishing the job. Upstairs were four bedrooms and a small bathroom. It was a good thing Mum and Dad had their six kids ten years apart, otherwise we would have been stepping over each other.

The main floor was comprised of a living, family room, and kitchen. We had a small pantry and a trap door in the worn wood floor, and six wooden steps, hanging on for dear life, led down to a mud cellar.

My family was working class poor. We managed to keep from going hungry by keeping a vegetable garden on the top of the hill behind our house. Potatoes went a long way in our household. We stored them in the little mud cellar below the house. Rats? We had those too.

It was a mild Saturday evening in May, and we were sitting at the kitchen table having dinner.

"Mum is there enough stew for seconds?" Kevin asked.

"You know the rules, Kev." Mum chuckled.

"Finish first. Eat twice," Rob and I chorused.

Dad laughed as he poured the rest of his beer in his glass mug. A breeze fluttered through the window curtains. Dad sniffed the air a few times. "I can smell those cows grazing by the pond all the way from here."

"I don't smell anything," Mum said.

Kevin stuck his nose up and took a big sniff. "I smell it too, Dad."

Rob and I both stood up and sniffed. "It smells like rotting poo," Rob announced.

Kevin and I giggled. Rob was five and the baby of the family. He loved saying words like *poo* and *pee*.

"Well, whatever it is, I hope it goes away," Dad said, rising from the table with his beer mug. He strolled to the living room and eased himself down on his beige recliner. Grampy Dos found it at a church bazaar the year before. Practically brand new, he declared, when he drove up in his blue pickup truck and helped Dad carry it into the house.

It was Dad's favourite chair. "Good for watching TV," Dad would always say. Although every time he pressed down on the lever to put his feet up, he'd be snoring ten minutes later.

"That smell is even worse over here," Dad said.

"Well, maybe the boys can take a walk over to Morice's Mill Pond, see what's going on over there. Maybe one of the cows is sick or something," Mom said as she cleared the table. "Boys, help me finish up here first, then you can go."

"Can I have some ice cream, Mummy?" Rob asked.

"Honey, we don't have any ice cream in the freezer. Maybe next week after Mum and Dad get paid, okay?"

Rob's face fell. He was still too young to understand.

"Hey Rob, wanna go for a piggyback ride?" I asked him.

Rob's eyes lit up, and he bobbed his head. He stood up in his chair, and I turned my back and hunched over so he could climb on. "Make sure you hang on tight," I said as I began to trot around like a horse.

I galloped into the living room around Dad's chair.

"Damn, if that stink hasn't gotten worse." Dad said. "What the hell is going on?" He stood up and turned his face into the corduroy fabric of the recliner. "I think it's this chair," Dad said. "C'mon boys, help me take this thing apart."

Kevin joined us and the three of us held helped Dad turned the chair over. We held onto the tufted headrest as Dad pulled back the fuzzy fabric covering the metal slats at the back.

"Jesus, Mary, and Joseph," Dad said.

"Mom! Come quick," Kevin yelled.

"What's the matter?" Mum came bustling out of the kitchen, wiping her soapy hands on a dish towel.

"Look at this," Dad said, holding his nose.

We all held our noses and leaned in.

Curled around one of the metal slats was a dead rat.

Mum said one of us kids had probably left the door open in the floor leading down to the cellar, and of course, Mr. Rat had probably crawled up and made his way to the cozy recliner. Maybe he got stuck or suffocated. Or maybe he just crawled in there to die.

I will never forget that smell. It is forever embedded in my nose. Every time I smell something rotten, I think back to that poor dead rat. To our house with no number. The old house where the nuns used to live. The house with the trap door leading down to a dirt cellar where we kept our potatoes for the winter, along with a few rats.

I have very strong memories of growing up in that house. Many of those memories were good. A lot of them weren't. I'm no different than many of you. We didn't all have perfect childhoods. Even if your family had money, you might have experienced emotional or physical abuse or neglect as a child.

Every child deserves to be cared for in a warm and comfortable home with good food and gifts on birthdays and special holidays. Every child deserves to feel safe in their home. Every child deserves to be nurtured and loved.

I grew up in a loving home, but that love wasn't always expressed in a "Brady Bunch" kind of way. Sometimes it was hard to recognize it. Other times it was weighed down with fear and shame.

My father, David, was a tough man. He dropped out of school in Grade 6. My mom quit in Grade 7. They quit so they could start working. They always worked, but they never could get ahead. Mom worked for Nortel on the assembly line, making phones. Dad worked for Maloney Electric in the factory, coiling the transformers and boxing them up for the guys who would climb the poles to install them. It was physically exhausting work that paid just over minimum wage—he made just over seven bucks an hour. I knew that wasn't much.

One day dad handed me a dollar and 21 cents.

"Don't tell your mother," he said. "Don't tell your brothers."

The dollar and 21 cents was the exact cost of a Happy Meal after tax. It was Dad's coffee money for the week. He gave me that money so I could eat the same thing as the other kids after our monthly tournaments, and he did it every month. He would take me aside, whisper to me that he had something to give me, count out the change, and drop it into my palm.

Dad showed me he loved me by giving me that money each time. It was his way of telling me he cared. Although I don't know what made me feel worse—knowing he was sacrificing that money so I could be one of the gang, or knowing he understood I would feel ashamed and embarrassed if I didn't have that money. He also didn't want another dad to pay for my Happy Meal because that would make *him* feel embarrassed. He understood the shame, because he felt it too.

The money was for the Happy Meal, but there was nothing happy about it for me. It was just a way for me to cover up my shame of being poor. It was an extravagance we couldn't afford, but I took the money anyway, because I wanted to pretend I was like every other kid on the team, at least on the surface.

I was motivated by shame, and along with that shame came a feeling of guilt for taking money that my dad needed. The guilt burned in my chest and further fueled my shame about who I was and where I came from. It was a toxic, endless loop.

Shame is a powerful feeling. Shame and guilt are doom and gloom twins. And those two feelings together can drown you in despair.

After our team ate at McDonalds, our bus driver, Fred, would drive us home. His nickname was "Cabbage Head Fred" because he had a big head. We never called him that. But that's what other people called him. I don't think he minded. Fred was a good guy.

"Hey, Fred, can you drop me off at Gerry's?" I asked him that first time.

"Sure thing, kiddo," Fred replied.

It was officially called Middle Sackville Variety, but everyone knew it as "Gerry's" because that was the owner's name. A squat, square building with a beige façade, it had two windows on one side of the door and one window on the other. Gerry always displayed something tempting like a new flavour of gum or candy—the kind that pop and fizz when it hit your tongue. Gerry's was the "everything" store. From lightbulbs to smokes to Jos Louis snack cakes, you could probably find it at Gerry's.

"Yeah, I'm kinda hungry," I said, perching on the seat across from Fred. No one ever sat beside the bus driver, unless you were old or a kid with no friends. "I'll think I'll get a bag of chips or something, and then walk home."

"I can wait for you, if you want, Timmy."

"Nah, that's okay, Gerry'll probably wanna hear about the game."

Fred threw me a grin over his shoulder. "Gerry always wants to know the score. He'll be talking about it all week, I'm sure."

The snack changed from week to week. Some weeks it was a chocolate bar, other weeks it was chips or gum. Fred never questioned me. He always had a smile and a laugh about Gerry.

But the truth was, I wasn't hungry, and I didn't have any change left for chips or even candy. If anyone tells you that lying makes things easier, it doesn't. Over time, I got better at it, but every time I lied, I had to wonder if it changed me somehow. Lying began to erode what was real for me, deep down to my core. Maybe that's why my stomach would tie itself into so many knots that it made me want to throw up. The real part of me was getting smaller and smaller, and the fake part was getting bigger and bigger.

Lying had become second nature to me. After all, if I could lie to everyone at my school about knowing David Sears after I won the trophy, it was nothing to lie about why I wanted to be dropped off at Gerry's. I lied to save face.

Fred knew exactly where I lived. The old house with no number, where the nuns used to live. But he never said anything. He just dropped me off in front of Gerry's, and then I would trudge the rest of the way home, hauling my skates—with the laces tied to form a loop—over one shoulder and my uniform and gear in my hockey bag over my other shoulder. I didn't want the other kids to see my house. They knew where I lived too, but I didn't want them to see.

Now, imagine a childhood full of moments like that. Shameful moments that added to my burden of guilt.

I'm not asking for your sympathy; I know you've had things to feel shame and guilt for too. I want to make a point about how heavy a burden shame and guilt can become if we don't deal with it; if we don't free ourselves from it so that we can live more productive and happy lives. These memories from our childhoods can fester, like that rat in Dad's recliner. They can build up over time and keep us from growing as individuals.

When I began to Own My Shit, it took me a year

to work through my own self-forgiveness. I did a lot of reading, and thinking, and talking to my family. Forgiveness is not about absolution. It's about acknowledgement. It's about making room in your psyche for motivation and change.

One of the most important lessons I have learned is that learning never stops. I was a pretty good student, but I never LOVED school. When I started on this path, however, I figured out how much I love to learn. I read as much as I can: books that inspire me; books that challenge my way of thinking; books that help me grow. In addition to the late Dr. Susan Jeffers, other authors I admire include Brendon Burchard, Stephen Covey, John C. Maxwell, Simon Sinek, Robin Sharma. I also admire Doctor Mike Evans—his videos (you can watch them on YouTube) gave me the initial boost I needed to make physical activity a part of my life. Every. Single. Day.

Learning has helped me do some serious housecleaning in my head—and to finally toss out that metaphorical rat in the recliner.

Chapter 4

Turn Lack of Awareness into a Self-awakening.

"Why don't you just count on yourselves?"
— The Great Gazoo

"It's a Gazoo episode!" I shouted with excitement as Kevin, Rob, and I huddled around the TV to watch *The Flintstones* one Saturday morning. *The Flintstones* was my favourite cartoon as a kid. It was originally broadcast from 1960 to 1966, but it became a huge hit with kids in North America as it was constantly and consistently re-broadcast for years after that. Set in the stone-age, the main characters, Fred and Barney, usually got into trouble in every episode, but there was always a "happy ending" or a lesson to be learned.

My favourite character was the Great Gazoo. He was a tiny, green, floating alien creature, banished from his advanced, futuristic, home planet Zetox to pre-historic planet Earth. He was forced into exile because he'd invented a doomsday machine just for the fun of it. In order to make amends and earn his way back home, Gazoo was required to do good deeds for the person(s) who discovered him. Of course, Fred and Barney, were the first to encounter Gazoo after he crashed in Bedrock.

"I wish we had a Great Gazoo," Robbie said, as he scooped up a spoonful of corn flakes.

"Yeah, if we had one, maybe we'd be rich," Kevin said biting into an apple.

"What would you do if you were rich, Tim?" Robbie asked me.

I sipped the last few drops of milk in my cereal bowl and thought for a moment. There were so many things I wished I had. A new bike, new skates, lots of toys . . . no more hand-me-down clothes. "If I were rich, I would buy us a big house with no rats in the cellar."

"Yeah, Mom and Dad would be so happy," Kevin said.

"And everything would be so good," Robbie added.

For the next half hour, my brothers and I snorted with laughter as Fred and Barney got themselves into mishap after mishap because they didn't listen to what Gazoo was truly telling them.

But I listened.

And I knew that if I had my own Gazoo, I wouldn't mess it up like Fred and Barney did.

Later, as we walked over to Grampy's house to take him some leftover stew that Mom had made, I couldn't help but think about Robbie's question. I wished I had my own Gazoo. I could make us all rich, and everything would be perfect. Money solved every problem, didn't it?

If I were rich, I wouldn't have been so scared to win the David Sears Trophy. I would have felt like I deserved it. I wouldn't have been so nervous about walking up to the podium in the gymnasium when I won the trophy, worrying about my hand-me-down pants with the tear in the crotch. I wouldn't have lied to the teacher about knowing David Sears. Dad wouldn't have had to give me a dollar and 21 cents each week for the McDonald's Happy Meal. I wouldn't have had to lie to Fred the bus driver about being hungry for a snack and asking him to drop me off at Gerry's.

We would be living in a clean new house with a real basement instead of a mud cellar with potatoes that we kept in a cardboard box and rats that snuck upstairs and got trapped in Dad's used recliner. The kind of basement with the cool wood panelling and maybe even a stereo and another TV. Dad could have bought a brand-new Lazy Boy to replace the old one that Gramps had given us. And Mom would be able to stop smoking because she wouldn't be so worried all the time about money and stuff.

If I'd only had a real Gazoo, I could have made us all rich and happy. But I could still do that right? I could still become rich. Lots of people started with nothing and then struck it rich. If I made it into the NHL, I could be really rich. I'd be famous too, and everyone would look up to me.

Gazoo had a big impact on me as a kid. I began to think of my own inner voice as the Great Gazoo. I loved the idea of having a magical creature in my life that could snap their fingers and make everything better. Isn't that what the fairy tales taught us? But I knew the reality of my situation. The only way for me to be happy was to make my own money. And lots of it. Then I could do whatever I wanted in life.

Forty years later, I knew the untruth of that. Money does not buy happiness the way they say. It can buy you physical comfort but not emotional peace. It can't make you escape that gnawing anxiety inside you. It can't make you stop smoking or drinking or binge eating. You can have all the money in the world, and it can't change your outlook. Sure, you can plunk down thirty thousand dollars to stay at a swanky health spa for a week, but unless YOU make the commitment to change, sooner or later you'll go back to overeating or drinking or smoking or taking drugs.

Gazoo has stayed with me. The idea of a voice whispering in your ear is one that intrigues me. Since I began to Own My Shit, I developed my own inner Gazoo-voice, but I learned to make it stronger and to trust its truth. Because remember the truth of the Great Gazoo? His driving force was to do good deeds so that he could earn his way home. What does that translate to in real life? Well, it's not much different is it? Being a good person every day so you can live a happy life. I'll take that.

One of the most important takeaways from Gazoo that I figured out is the idea that we can be motivated to change for the right reasons. Gazoo needed to do good deeds to get back home. Before I began to Own My Shit, my driving force was money. But when I began to change, I realized that my driving force had changed too. Remember the Four Foundations I talked about at the beginning of this book?
1. *Health/Wellness*
2. *Relationships*
3. *Money/Career*
4. *Spirituality*

I was only getting one of those right—number three. But just because I had done well in my work and was making money didn't mean I was happy or feeling successful in my life. As I said, I was 70 pounds overweight, I was a chain smoker, and I drank too much—and all of that was impacting my relationships with Annie, Cole and Sidnee. I didn't feel happy or in balance.

Oh, I could be the life of the party, but that was all for show. Inside I was miserable. And I certainly didn't feel a sense of greater purpose to reach outside myself and do something positive in society. My spirituality needed a major Great Gazoo overhaul.

What happens when you open a window in a dark, stuffy room? You let in light and fresh air. That's what happened to me when I "opened the window" to Annie after the hockey game on that fateful night of January 3, 2012. The next day, I shared what I was going through with Cole and Sidnee and let in a fresh breeze. I began to delve into the reasons I'd been abusing food, cigarettes, and alcohol, and I began to realize that my feelings of disconnectedness from my life were rooted in the past. In my childhood.

When I figured out what had been haunting me since I was a kid—when I learned to let go of the pain and shame of living in a broken-down house with no number, a tarp on one side, and rats in the mud cellar—I began to reconnect to my life and my family. I began to see my career differently, as well. I discovered that I loved my job because it was fulfilling and not because I made a lot of money doing it.

When I began to embrace that little kid again—

that kid who wanted so much to play for the NHL but who never got the chance, that kid who lost his way when he was a teenager and then had to find his way back—then I truly began to feel like I was home.

When I took responsibility for my destructive actions and the impact that my behaviour had on my family, that's when I realized that I could begin to find the balance in those four parts of my life.

When I began to truly Own My Shit, I began to heal.

Now I am fully aware of my own Great Gazoo. That little voice inside me that lets me know when I'm on the right path or when I need to make a shift. I listen to my Great Gazoo and I like what he has to say.

Try this exercise, either on your laptop or on paper. Think back to a movie, book, TV show, or song from your childhood.

How did that song or movie resonate with you?

How did you feel when you watched that TV show or movie?

Has it stayed with you today?

Do you find comfort in it?

Has it helped get you through tough times throughout your life? How?

Chapter 5

Our Parents Made Their Mistakes.
We Will Make Ours.

"Experience is simply the name
we give our mistakes."
— Oscar Wilde

"If you ever steal anything, I'll fuckin' kill you."

Dad grabbed me by the collar and gave me a shake that made my teeth rattle. I stared at him with wide eyes. My knees were shaking so hard, they sounded like sticks clacking together.

"B-but I didn't do nothin'," I squeaked out.

"And it better stay that way, Timmy." Dad leaned in close, so close that the beer fumes from his breath were making me dizzy.

"I may not have jack shit when it comes to money or a fancy house. But the name David Richardson means something in this town. My reputation, son. My reputation."

I may have been a liar, but I wasn't a thief. It was all thanks to Dennis Lorette, who'd swiped a box of fishing lures and a pack of cigarettes from Gerry's. Dennis was the town daredevil. He wasn't afraid of anything. Once he found an old door someone left in the trash and dragged it home. Then he rolled an empty barrel down the street to the bottom of the hill and lay the rotting door against it as a makeshift ramp. Then he leapt on his bike and pedaled up the hill, turned the bike around, and with a loud whoop, rode down the hill as fast as the wind. He hit the ramp and flew so high, he almost hit a bird. Then he landed on the grass and let out another yell. Me and my brothers had seen it all. We were just getting home from Grampy's house, and Mum told us we better not get it into our heads to do what Dennis just did.

Dennis was a wild kid and ended up a heavy smoker and drinker. He died of throat cancer, just shy of his 50th birthday. I often wonder how it might have been if only he'd been able to harness that wild and exuberant spirit. Who knows how he might have turned out?

I certainly wasn't wild like Dennis. I did some stupid things in my childhood, but I knew inherently that pulling stunts wouldn't get me far in life.

"Am I making myself clear, son?"

Dad stretched to his full height, his hand continuing to rest heavily on my shoulder.

"Yes, sir."

"And you'll never steal anything, will you?"

"No, sir."

I never did.

I never forgot that lesson Dad taught me. My dad could be funny and kind, but he could also be harsh. I learned from that experience. But I carried that fear inside me. I feared my dad.

Fear is not a good feeling to carry with you when you're a kid. If you're afraid of one or both of your parents, then how can you grow and thrive? Maybe Dennis had parents who were too permissive, or maybe they just didn't know what he was up to half the time. When you're a kid, you have no say in anything. All I knew was, I better not steal, or my dad would beat the crap out of me.

When Sidnee and Cole were born, I vowed never to instill that kind of fear in them. I was never harsh or mean. I was determined never to parent my kids the way my dad parented me.

"Cole stole a pack of gum today at the store," Annie whispered to me as she drizzled olive oil and balsamic vinegar dressing over the salad.

"Oh geez," I whispered back, cutting up grilled chicken breast into bite—sized pieces for the kids. I looked over at the kids, who were sprawled in front of the TV in the family room area, watching an old episode of the Flintstones. I couldn't help it. I was such a fan of the show when I was a kid that I owned all the original episodes on DVD.

"I found it after we got home," Annie went on. "It was in his pocket."

"Did you ask him where he got it?" I asked.

"He said he didn't know," she replied, concern in her eyes. "Sidnee kept grabbing things off the shelves, maybe Cole thought it was okay to do that?"

"Mommy! Daddy!" four-year-old Sidnee shouted. She ran up to us, her hazel eyes wide and her soft blonde hair making a halo around her cherubic face. "Cole thed he's gonna make me dith-apear like Gweat Gazoo!"

Annie and I glanced at each other and tried not to burst out laughing. Our children were always keeping us on our toes.

"Honey," Annie said reassuringly. "I promise you that Cole cannot make you disappear."

"Besides," I added. "Gazoo is pretty cool and has all those powers—so Cole couldn't make *you* disappear. Only you would have the power to do that."

"I could gwow up to be Gweat Gazoo?" she asked in an awed whisper.

"You can be anything you want to be, sweetheart," I said, picking her up and twirling her around in a circle. She squealed in delight. "In fact, I know that when you grow up, you'll be even greater than the Great Gazoo."

After dinner, Annie and I decided that I would take Cole back to the grocery store the next day to return the pack of gum and apologize. Cole was just five years old, but he was old enough to learn a major life lesson.

I recalled my father's harsh lecture when I was a boy. I refused to go down that road. For Dad, teaching me a lesson meant ordering me not to do something because there would be hell to pay if his reputation got sullied in any way. But I wanted to teach my son that stealing is wrong, and that had nothing to do with my reputation. It wasn't about me and my ego, it was about how I could help build Cole's self-esteem instead of cutting him down. Then an idea came to me.

The next day I drove Cole back to the store. The gum felt like a lead weight in my pocket. We walked into the store, and I stopped and crouched down so I was at eye level with Cole. I pulled out the pack of gum and showed it to Cole.

"Did you take this pack of gum yesterday, son?"

He shrugged his little shoulders, his hazel eyes skittering away from mine.

"Cole, you know it's against the law to steal, right?"

Cole's face scrunched up. "What's the law, Daddy?"

"It means it's wrong to take something that's not yours. The police will arrest you and put you in jail for that."

"Jail?" My son's eyes widened. "That doesn't sound like a good place."

I suppressed a smile. I knew I was getting through. I decided to take it a step further.

"Okay, we need to talk to the security guard." I took Cole's hand and we walked to the customer service desk. I explained to them what was going on and asked them to inform the guard about my idea.

Five-year-olds have fidgeting down to a fine art, and by the time the guard arrived forty-five minutes later, Cole was about ready to do a back flip off the chair.

The security guard shot me a quick wink then turned to Cole and regarded him in silence for a few moments. He was tall and beefy and had a shaved head. He was perfect.

"What seems to be the problem, here?" the security guard asked in a gruff voice.

"Well, Mr. Policeman, my son Cole here has something to tell you."

"What do you want to say to me, young man?" The guard put his hands on his hips and tapped his foot.

"I—I" Cole glanced at me, his hazel eyes round like saucers. I nodded encouragement. Cole handed the pack of gum to the security guard and said. "I—I took this."

"Oh, you mean you stole this pack of gum?" the guard asked.

Cole nodded solemnly.

"Son, do you know what happens when people steal?" the guard asked, crossing his arms in front of his chest.

Cole swallowed and took a step closer to me, grabbing my pant leg. "They go to jail, sir?"

"They go to jail, yes," the guard replied.

I crouched down beside my son and put my hand on his shoulders and looked him straight in the eye. "Cole, if you go to jail, don't you worry, I promise to visit you as often as I can." At this point Cole's lips were trembling and I knew we'd made our point. "Cole, do you think you should apologize for stealing the gum?"

"I'm sorry, Mr. Policeman. I won't never steal gum forever n' ever."

The security guard bent down and offered Cole his hand. Cole took it and they shook hands. "You are an impressive boy," the guard said. "Not many kids could do what you just did."

"Did you hear that, Cole?" I said. "Mr. Policeman is congratulating you for telling the truth and owning up to your mistake. It's not an easy thing to do."

"How come it's not easy?" Cole asked as he wiped his nose with the back of his hand.

"Because it's hard to admit when you're wrong. It's hard to say sorry. And most of all, it's hard to make things right. But you know what Cole? You did all of those things. And I'm so proud of you. I love you, Cole."

"I love you too, Daddy."

I hugged my son tight and released a deep breath when my son hugged me back.

As I drove us home, I realized I had been just as worried as my son back there at the store. Staying calm and keeping things on a "lighter" level was the right approach.

My dad certainly got through to me all those years ago by threatening me with physical violence if I didn't comply. Was the fear of getting a beating by my dad all that different from the fear of getting thrown into jail? Is fear a motivator at all? Looking back, I know that what I did was not aggressive or physically violent, which is what I had learned as a boy, but it had instilled fear all the same. There were times over the years that I used fear as a motivator with my own kids. And I'm not proud of it.

I was able to learn from my own past, but had I let it go? It would take me a few years to figure that out. To figure out the difference between the lessons my parents had taught me and the values I wanted to live by. My parents hadn't had it all wrong. They did the best they could with what knew. Their experiences growing up had shaped them. They made mistakes, but they also owned up to them. And maybe that was the biggest lesson I learned from my parents, to own up to your mistakes. Maybe the seeds of Own Your Shit had been planted all those years go in my own childhood. Sometimes you need a good mind shake in order to clear all those cobwebs from the past.

Chapter 6

Never Quit. Own Your Shit.

"Bad habits are easier to abandon
today than tomorrow."
— *Yiddish Proverb*

"Dad, did you know that cigarettes have rat poison in them?"

"No, Timmy, but I wish I did, because I'd still have my recliner."

Laughter bubbled around the dinner table.

"Dad, rats can't smoke cigarettes," Rob giggled as he speared a chunk of hot dog from his bowl of baked beans.

"Don't forget to eat the beans too, Robbie," Mum said, breaking a piece of bread and sopping up the tomato sauce.

It was a cool Friday night in October, and we were all feeling relaxed because tomorrow was Saturday, and we could sleep in an extra hour. I turned to Mum and patted her hand to get her attention. I didn't think Dad would care much about what I'd learned at school that day, but maybe Mum would. "Mum, they also have that same stinky stuff that's in moth balls. Like the ones you use in the wooden box where you keep Grammy's good tablecloth."

"Ewwww! Those are so stinky." Kevin held his nose.

"They may be stinky, but they do their job," Mum said.

"But Mum, maybe it's not good to smoke," I said.

"You know what, Timmy?" Mum tapped the table top with her index finger. "I think you're right. I think it's not good to smoke. Would you be happy if I quit?"

We all yelled in excitement.

"How are you gonna do it, Mum?" I asked, kicking my chair happily.

"Well now, I'll just stop buying cigarettes," she said.

"But how, Mum?" Kevin chimed in.

"I can do it. Just like that." She snapped her fingers, and Dad burst into laughter.

"I'll believe it when I see it." Dad got up from the table and pulled out his own pack of cigarettes. He waved it around in the air. "You've been smoking all your life. You've tried quitting cold turkey before, what makes you think you can do it now?"

I turned to Mum, hopeful. She looked at me and winked.

"I think I can do it. And besides, we can save that extra bit of money for something special." She said it like it was a piece of cake. She had no trouble stopping. It was all about will power and just making that decision and sticking to it. I was so proud of Mom.

Two weeks later, I had to ask permission from

Mom for an upcoming school field trip to the Maritime Museum of Atlantic Canada in Halifax, Nova Scotia. Keep in mind Middle Sackville is on the border of New Brunswick and Nova Scotia, so heading over to Halifax wasn't far. When I got home after school, Kevin said Mum had gone to fill up the gas tank at John Ayer's Gas Station, next to Gerry's variety store. I hopped on my bike and pedaled along to meet up with her there. Mum would often chat a few minutes with John after he finished filling up the tank, so I figured she would be there a while. But when I got there, I saw something that left me gobsmacked. Mum was standing beside John, chatting and puffing away on a cigarette as he filled up the tank. I got off my bike and stomped up to her.

"You lied!" I yelled. My lips were trembling, and I was blinking so hard, it was all I could do to keep my tears from flowing down my cheeks.

The colour drained from my mother's face. She looked like she'd been caught robbing a bank. I didn't wait for her to reply. I leapt on my bike and raced as far away from Mum as I could get.

I didn't realize it at the time because I was too young, but my mother was taking a huge risk lighting up at a gas station. When I look back now, I just shake my head in wonder that she didn't blow herself and the entire place up. It goes to show you that in many ways, my family and I were lucky. Very lucky indeed. But we can't live our lives hoping for "blind luck" to bail us out of jams.

Owning Your Shit is all about taking responsibility, not just for yourself but everyone around you. By lighting up a cigarette at a gas station, my mom was not only risking her own life, but the lives of everyone else around her—including the young son who'd caught her smoking.

I want you to take a moment and think back to your childhood—your youth, teen years, 20s—heck, even as recently as last week. Think back to a moment in your own life when you did something stupid and could have gotten someone killed if it were not for luck—or divine intervention or whatever you want to call it—stepping in and saving your dumb ass. Think back to your childhood, or college years, or your first job, or a party when you were sixteen, or when you were first learning to drive, or when some idiot double-dog-dared you. Think back, and I'm sure you can come up with at least two instances where you did something that put you, and potentially others, in danger, and yet somehow you managed to avoid the ultimate consequence.

Here's what I want you to do—just so you keep that memory (or memories) front and centre as we proceed. I want you to write down one example (or more if you have them) of instances where you did something that put your life and the lives of others at risk because you were NOT Owning Your Shit.

How old were you when it happened?

When did it happen?

What did you do?

As you reflect back on that incident or incidents, what comes to mind? Do you shake your head and wonder how in the heck you got away unscathed? Do you feel a sense of relief that it was a one-time only deal? Do you secretly feel proud of yourself for getting away with it? Well, you know what? Actions do have consequences. There are good risks and bad risks in life. Starting your own business is potentially a good risk (if you've done your prep) but getting into your car after chugging six beers at a friend's party is a bad risk. Thinking I could get into my car with my son after drinking at that hockey game in 2012 was a stupid risk.

My purpose is not to rap you on the knuckles, but to spark awareness so that you are mindful of your actions and what can happen with just one flick of ash from a cigarette. Any time you do something without being mindful of everyone and everything around you, you are taking a bad risk. Self-destructive actions can have tragic consequences. All you have to do is watch a few minutes of the news or flip through the newspaper or spend a few minutes scrolling through your Facebook feed. How many times have you read about a fire starting from a lit cigarette in a home where someone fell asleep? Why is it so hard for some of us to be mindful? To be aware of our actions and possible consequences?

When we allow destructive habits to control us, we cannot make thoughtful decisions. Smoking, drinking, and other such habits interfere with our ability to think clearly. Their very nature is to distract us from our thoughts. To enable us to "lose ourselves" by lifting that cigarette to our mouths and taking a puff, or by lifting that glass of beer or wine to our lips and taking a sip.

Being aware and mindful—being *present*—gives us the clarity we need to deal with stressful situations head-on instead of avoiding the pain in our lives by numbing ourselves into incoherence. It sounds like common sense, doesn't it? The trouble is, common sense can escape us when we don't practice Owning Our Shit.

The day I caught Mum in her lie, she found me a while later, sitting on the hill behind our house, where we planted the garden that kept us going throughout the fall and winter. I pretended I didn't know she was there as I continued to scoop up handfuls of soil and let the granules sift through my fingers. She plopped herself down beside me and was quiet for a few minutes. We both sat there staring out across Morice's Mill Pond and beyond, to Silver Lake.

"I'm sorry," she eventually said in a splintered voice. "I shouldn't have lied to you, Timmy. I was having a hard time sticking to my promise and I—I slipped up a couple of times."

I looked up at her, and her eyes were swimming with tears.

"Okay," she went on, "I slipped up a lot of times. I know I don't deserve your forgiveness, but if you could see it in your heart to forgive me, I promise to try harder, and I won't lie to you again. If I mess up again, I promise to tell you. OK?"

"You're really sorry, aren't you Mum?" I asked her. I guess I was crying too, because she wrapped her arms around me and hugged me tight.

"Yes, I am really sorry, Timmy." She pulled back and combed my hair out of my eyes. "I let you down, and that's not right. It's not right at all."

"Mum, why didn't you tell us you were having trouble quittin' cold turkey?"

"I . . ." She paused for a moment then released a deep sigh. "Sometimes it's hard to admit when you fail at something. I didn't want to let you down. You were so proud of me. I liked having you proud of me, Timmy."

"But Mum, why? I'm just a kid."

"Just a kid?" She hugged me again. "You kids are everything to me. If you're not proud of me, then how can I be proud of myself?"

It was at that moment that I learned something important about my mom. She showed me that being able to admit the truth of a failure is more important than succeeding. She showed me the difference between shame and humility. Shame is what made her lie about her smoking. Humility is what allowed her to apologize to me about lying.

It would be many years before I figured out one more thing. To my mom, admitting failure to me was worse that the failure itself. When you fail at something and no one knows except you, it's easier to push it away. To hide it in a dusty, old trunk in a secret corner of the darkest part of your soul. But as we keep failing and keep falling, we keep filling that trunk. How much despair do you think you can fit in there?

It's hard to fail. But it's even harder to tell a loved one that you failed. That life lesson became a moment of truth in my own life, when I had to own up to my own self-destructive behaviour, and when I had to face my own lies.

My mother's entire self-worth came from how we saw her. She needed to be perceived as strong and able. Not weak, and certainly not a failure. I wish my mom had had the other kind of self-esteem. The kind that's embedded into your very fibre. The kind that stays with you no matter what. I wish she'd been able to tell me about that kind of self-worth. But Mum didn't know about it, and neither did I. It would take me a few decades to comprehend it, and it wasn't until I began to Own My Shit that I truly felt it in my very being.

Owning Your Shit isn't just about getting rid of those bad habits, like excessive drinking, smoking, or eating. It's about realizing that you are worthy enough and matter enough to not need those constructed mind-numbing actions in the first place. Self-destructive behaviour only serves to undermine your belief in in your true worth. It erodes it until it vanishes completely. Owning Your Shit is about being aware every day that your health and well-being are worth it—that *you* are worth it.

Chapter 7

Determination is a Super Power.

"Gold medals aren't really made of gold.
They're made of sweat, determination,
and a hard-to-find alloy called guts."
— Dan Gable

Thump. Thump. Thump. Thump.

I felt the pounding in my heart, pumping blood through my veins.

Thump. Thump. Thump. Thump.

I heard the pounding of my feet, propelling me forward to the finish line.

I threw a quick glance over my shoulder, but I couldn't see anyone.

I was all alone on the road.

Mile 15. I flew by the marker.

One mile to go.

A car pulled up on my right side and proceeded to keep pace. The window rolled down.

"The runner behind you just passed marker fourteen. You're doing great, son!" Dad shouted from the car.

I was exhausted, but those words buoyed my

spirit. Dad was there. He was right there by my side.

He passed me a paper cup of water. My parched throat welcomed the cool liquid. I gulped it down and tossed it back to my dad. I didn't want to slow down. I didn't want to break stride, or I would probably topple to the pavement.

"Don't drink so fast, or you might get sick."

"Okay, Dad."

"You're gonna win this Timmy. You've got it in the bag."

The sun beat down on my head on that hot September day.

I wanted to win. I wanted to win so badly. I had to keep reminding myself that I was running for a good cause, The Sackville Walkathon to raise money for the Canadian Cancer Society.

The race began at Mount Allison University and wound its way along Main Street. It was a popular event and generally drew 500 participants every year. I began taking part in the Walkathon when I was eleven years old, with my mom and Robbie and Kevin. We signed up as many sponsors as we could to raise as much money as possible. That was the whole point of the event, right? But something happened that first year. As I walked along the route with Mum and my brothers, a young guy sped right by us—a university student at Mount Allison. He ended up winning, crossing the finished line first and getting the trophy. He hadn't walked like the rest of us. He ran the entire way.

I decided that the next year, I would run it too. I began training every day. I ran every morning. I didn't really know what I was doing, but I figured it was just like hockey. You had to practice every day in order to get better and faster. And it was good exercise for hockey as well. I just made the decision and did it. Ironic, isn't it? When I was a kid, I had that sense of commitment for Owning Your Shit. I felt in my core. *Make a decision to make a decision and never negotiate with yourself.* I did that at the age of 12. I decided I would run that marathon and I knew that in order to do so, I would have to train every day.

How did I know that? Why did I know that? Well, just like the Great Gazoo, we all have inner wisdom inside us, we just have to listen. When we Own Our Shit, we are paying attention to that inner voice.

I didn't love running every day. Some days, I just wanted to sleep in. But I loved the feeling of accomplishment after a run. I loved feeling the wind at my back. I loved knowing that my legs were taking me farther and farther with each passing week. I loved the sense of freedom that coursed through me as I ran.

The next year, at the age of 12, I entered again and ran it as a race. I wanted to win. I wanted to win so badly—but I came third, and I was crushed. There was no question in my mind about what I needed to do. I Owned My Shit. I continued to train every day. I entered again when I was 13 and I won. I went on to win again at the age of 14 and 15. The organizers ended up giving me the trophy and basically retiring it.

I had been determined to win. I trained hard and I won. It was a huge thrill for me. I realized that when I trained hard at something, I usually ended up winning. Was that what life about? Work hard and you will be successful? But my mom and dad worked hard, and they weren't successful. We lived in a house with no number and a tarp on one side. We had rats in our basement. Heck, it wasn't even a basement, it was a mud cellar with a trap door. I wore hand-me-downs to school that were ten years old. My dad counted out every last penny of the dollar and 21 cents he gave me each week to get a Happy Meal after practice. No, working hard wasn't enough. You had to do more than work hard. You had to win. You had to win at everything you did.

As a child, I understood Own Your Shit, when it came to commitment and drive. But I didn't understand when it came to purpose. Own Your Shit is not about winning. It's about tapping into your purpose in life. It's not about the finish line, it's about the race—the process to your purpose. The journey itself is key. The journey is more important than the destination.

But back then, winning was everything. If I didn't win, then I wouldn't be successful. Hard work was part of it, but so was the drive to win, because I was certain that's what made the difference. I didn't want to end up like my parents, living in a house with no number. I wanted to be a winner. And I had to do everything I could to get there.

But when I became financially successful, I didn't feel like a winner. I felt like the biggest loser on the planet. I was miserable. I was obese. I was a functioning alcoholic, and I was a heavy smoker. How could I have been so wrong? Success wasn't about winning. Being successful means pursuing balance in the four key quadrants of your life that I mentioned earlier—relationships, career/financial, health, and spirituality. Finding balance in all those areas is what Owning your Shit truly means. As a child, I had figured out part of that, but I had a lot more "training" to do before I figured out the rest.

Think back to a time when you won a trophy or an award. Or when you accomplished a tough project. Or when you graduated from high school or college or university. How did you feel at the moment it was over? Sure, you were happy. You were excited. You were proud of yourself. But weren't you also thinking about the next step? What you were going to do next? See, that's where the magic is. The magic in life is in the doing. It's in the practicing. It's in the commitment to something every day. It's in the working of your daily life. It's not about winning. It's about what you did to get there. That's the important part. That's the part we learn from. That's the part that gives us that sense of accomplishment. That's the part that inspires others.

You don't have to cross the finish line first.

You don't have to win the trophy.

You just have to get in the race.

Chapter 8

Between Life and Death.

*"Even death is not to be feared by one
who has lived wisely."*
—Buddha

Grampy scraped the sulphur match against the red striker on the back of the match book. Cupping the flame with his hand, he lit the wick in the oil lamp on the small wooden table beneath the shuttered window. A glow bloomed in the lamp and lit up the entire cabin, like something out of a Jack London adventure story.

"Grampy this is so cool!" I said, turning in a circle. Two bunk beds sat in one corner. In the centre of the room was a small wood stove.

It was a frigid February morning. Rabbit hunting season in New Brunswick typically starts in the fall and runs until early spring. Grampy always said that winter was the best time to hunt rabbits because you could see their tracks in the snow. There was no one better at hunting than my grandfather Dos. Grampy Dos knew everything about hunting and fishing. He drove around on his moped with a wooden box tied behind him and a hat on his head that said, "Gone Fishing." Grampy knew every fishing hole in the area and everything there was to know about surviving in the wilderness. I figured that was a lot because he'd been married three times, and Mum said he knew more about surviving in the woods than he did about marriage.

Grampy had been retired for as long as I could remember, which was a long time considering I was eleven years old, but he used to work as a molder at the Enterprise Foundry. I thought that was the coolest job ever. Mum and Dad told us that our area used to be one of the top places where they made cast iron stoves, and Grampy was one of the best at making them.

"We're going to have fun this weekend," Grampy said now as he placed a few small logs in the wood stove. In a matter of minutes, the cabin was warm and toasty. It was just after 2:00 p.m. on Friday, but Grampy wanted to get a head start setting out the snares to catch the rabbits.

"Have you got that sack of carrots I told you to pack?" Grampy asked.

I pulled out the bag from my back pack and set it on the scarred surface of the table. "Here it is, Grampy," I said, excited to get going.

Grampy went out to his pickup truck and came back a few minutes later with a cardboard box. He plunked it down on the table and began to take out the objects. Metal wire, an axe and pliers, and two pairs of work gloves. He showed me how to cut the wire and tie a loop that would catch the rabbit.

"Now, we have to gather some branches. Heavier long ones and smaller ones," he told me. As I gathered the wood and brought it back to Grampy, he began to hack off the needles on the branches, clearing a space in the middle of each. We then carried them in our bags farther into the clearings in the woods.

"See those little trails there?" Grampy asked me. I did. The trails were narrow, big enough for rabbits and other small woodland animals to pass along. "We're going to set up our traps along those kinds of trails. It's where the rabbits travel."

I nodded in excitement. Grampy was teaching me how to be a hunter, just like he'd taught others in our family. Now it was my turn. We set up the snares, setting the large branches across the rabbit path and shoving sticks into the snowdrifts down to the dirt so we could link the snare between them. Grampy also made an X shape with two smaller sticks below the wire loop, so the rabbit would have no choice but to go through the snare.

"You can't catch a bee without honey," Grampy said as he snapped off a bit of carrot and attached it to the wire.

That's how the rabbit would get caught.

Grampy and I set up about ten snares that afternoon and evening. By the time we were done, it was dark, and my stomach was growling.

"I think it's time for dinner." Grampy grinned and patted me on the back. "You did good today, Timmy."

"Thanks, Grampy." His compliment made me happy. It wasn't every day you got a compliment from someone in my family, but when you did, it was well-earned.

"Do you think we'll catch a bunch of rabbits tonight?"

"Well, we'll see. We'll check the traps in the morning. Hopefully, we'll have a few rabbits, and then we can make rabbit stew tomorrow for dinner."

Grampy pulled a container out of the cooler. Inside were several sandwiches—chopped egg and ham—along with apples and even chocolate chip cookies. Grampy had water for me and a ginger ale for himself.

"Grampy, how come you know all this stuff?" I asked, munching on a chunk of apple.

He took off his cap and scratched his head as though he were pondering my question.

"Well, when I was your age, I had no choice. I had to learn how to survive. It wasn't as easy as it is nowadays when you can drive to the store and buy food."

"You mean you didn't have any stores?"

"Oh, we had stores, but not like today. Not these big grocery stores that have everything you could ever want. I didn't live in a big city like Toronto. I had to learn how to shoot, and hunt, and fish."

"But we don't have to learn all those things now, Grampy, because we have those big stores."

"That's true, but I think it's important to learn the old ways. What if something were to happen, and you'd have no choice but to make rabbit snares so you can eat and feed your family? In life, you have to do what you have to do. And if you know how to feed yourself, then that's an important lesson."

I nodded. Grampy was very old, so he knew what was what. Besides, he was the only grandparent I had, so I cherished my time with him.

The next day we ended up catching eight rabbits. When we got to the ninth snare, I gasped. The animal was still alive, struggling because his leg had been caught and he couldn't get loose. He was frantically chewing at the wire when we arrived, and blood had seeped into his white and grey fur where the wire had dug into his hind leg.

"Grampy! What are we gonna do?" I whispered.

"Sometimes this happens, but you gotta do what you gotta do." Grampy took his axe out and held it so that the flat part of the blade faced down, then he bent and reached for the squirming rabbit.

"EEEE!! EEEE!!!" The rabbit started to screech, its movements frantic now.

Grampy swung up and down, hitting rabbit's head with the flat of his axe.

"Eee!" The rabbit continued to screech, but now its cries were not as loud.

Grampy whacked the rabbit again.

"Eee…" The rabbit let out a little moan and then stopped struggling.

He was dead.

I began to tremble as I realized what I had just witnessed. Grampy had killed the rabbit. Grampy removed the snare and bagged the rabbit. His hands were stained with blood.

"Grampy, he was screaming, and you killed him," I said thickly, trying to hold back my tears.

Grampy sighed and wiped his hands on a cloth. "Timmy, that's what rabbit snares are meant to do. Kill rabbits."

"Y-yes but he wasn't dead. You killed him with your axe."

"He was suffering. His leg was caught in the trap. I put him out of his misery."

"But now we're gonna eat him." I took a deep

breath, feeling a wave of panic wash over me. I was shocked. Frozen. I had just watched my grandfather kill a wounded creature. I would never forget that agonized scream of *eee*.... How could I eat something that Grampy had killed in front of my very eyes? I couldn't hold back the tears any longer.

"Timmy, have you ever eaten rabbit stew before?"

"Y-yes," I said swiping at my eyes. "Mum makes it in the fall and winter."

"And do you like rabbit stew?"

"Yes..." I sniffled.

"And when your mum sets a bowl of hot rabbit stew with potatoes, onions, carrots, and gravy all mixed in, what do you do?

"I eat it."

"Yes, you eat it. And when you go grocery shopping with your mum, and she buys ground meat and makes chili for dinner, or meatballs and spaghetti, do you think about the cow that meat came from?"

"No, not really, because we just went to the store."

"So, you have no way of knowing how that cow lived before he died and then was turned into meat."

I shrugged not understanding what Grampy meant. "I guess he lived on a farm."

"Yes, I'm sure he did," Grampy went on. "He probably didn't have much room to move around. Unlike that rabbit. That rabbit had a good life hopping around the woods with his rabbit family and friends. We didn't catch him and put him in a cage for years. He lived a great life right up until his last moment. And you were a part of that life. Now he's going to be a part of you."

We walked back to the cabin. I understood what Grampy had said, but I still felt sad. I still needed to talk some more about the rabbit. I had to know something.

"Grampy, if we eat the rabbits, then how do they go to heaven?" I asked. That was the real question. I was an altar boy, after all. And I wanted to believe that everyone goes to heaven, except for bad people. But rabbits weren't bad. They were fluffy and cute, and we ate them in our stew. Where did they go?

"Have a seat, Timmy," Grampy left the sack of rabbits in the corner and rinsed his hands from the pail of water by the door. He dried them and then sat across from me. "We eat to survive. We need to eat. You need to eat to grow up strong so you can work and provide for your own family. I need to eat to stay alive."

"But what about the rabbits? What happens to them when we eat them?"

"What happens to us after we die?"

"We get buried and then our souls fly up to heaven."

"Ah, so your soul rises up to Heaven. It doesn't stay buried under ground."

"No. Everyone knows that." I rolled my eyes at Grampy. And he smiled.

"Then don't you think it's the same for rabbits? After I put that little fella out of his misery, his soul hopped up to heaven."

"Do you think so?"

"Of course, I do. I have faith, don't you?"

I sighed. "I'm scared about that, Grampy."

"Scared?" Grampy leaned in and tapped me on the nose. "Timmy, you have a long way to go before you get to my age. You have a lot of life to live. I'm an old man, and I'm not scared to die."

"How come?"

"Because I get to see my mother and father, my siblings, your Grammy. I get to see my friends. I get to see God. I get to be free of these old bones and I can run around like a kid again."

"Do you think you'll see the rabbit in Heaven?"

"I promise to look for him. But I'm sure he's fine."

I nodded solemnly.

Grampy opened the cooler and took out something wrapped in a cloth. He set it on the table and unwrapped it, revealing a loaf of dark, heavy bread. "We all return back to the earth, Timmy. I will. You will. Just like that rabbit." He cut two thick slices and then took out two more cloth-wrapped items. He unwrapped them and set out a triangle of cheddar and two more apples. "We all have our time to go. That's why we have to live life to the fullest while we're here. That rabbit had a good life hopping around and living in the woods with his animal friends." Slicing the cheddar and apples, he set everything out on the cloth and then poured us both a cup of water. "His bones will return to the earth. But his spirit will move on. We will eat that rabbit, and then, when it's our time to go, we will return to the earth and our spirits will move on too. The one thing we all have in common is that we all live, and we all die. But that doesn't mean we can't enjoy the time we have here."

"Grampy, I hope when I die, I'll see you again," I said around a mouthful of apple.

Grampy broke off a chunk of bread and laid a

slice of cheese on it. "Timmy, I hope you live a very long life, full of happiness and good health. When you die a long time from now, I'm going to meet you in heaven, and I promise to take you fishing." He popped the bread and cheese in his mouth and winked at me.

I laughed at the funny face he made. Grampy spent the rest of the weekend telling me stories about his childhood, and I knew without a doubt that when I died, I would see him again and we would go fishing.

Decades have passed since that weekend in the woods hunting for rabbits, but I have carried my grandfather's stories and strength with me. In 2012, when I began to take a long hard look at my life and how it had gone off the rails. I remembered Grampy's spirit and his love of life. I remembered how important it is to live life to the fullest and not take one day for granted.

I want you to think about how you want to lead your life. Take a moment and think back to your childhood when you first found out or figured out about life and death. How did you feel about it back then? What event or person brought on the revelation? How did you feel about losing a loved one?

How do you feel about it now?

Chapter 9

Time Will Pass. How Do You Intend to Pass Your Time?

"Time is what we want most,
but what we use worst."
— William Penn

It was cold. So cold. I flipped back the blankets on my bed and pulled out the pile of clothes I'd hidden at the foot the night before. I was already wearing my grey wool socks, a Christmas present from Mum and Dad. Yanking on my bell-bottoms over my pajamas, I got up from my bed and tiptoed to the door, hoping the old wooden floorboards wouldn't creak

Creeeaaak!

"Hey, what are you doing up so early?" my brother Robbie grumbled from across the room. It was still dark, and I hadn't turned on the light.

"I'm going to Grampy's," I replied, as I tucked my pajama top into my waist band and put on my heavy blue sweater.

"For what?" Robbie asked

"The watch. Remember?"

Robbie yawned. "It's too cold. You're nuts."

"Maybe I am, but I'm gonna get that watch."

"I bet it's not even worth anything." Robbie yawned again. My eyes had adjusted to the dark room. The moonlight glinted off the snow and peeked in through the space between the curtain panels.

I glanced at the alarm clock. It was quarter to six on January first—New Year's Day. I was determined to be the first one at my grandfather's house. Grampy Dos was Mum's dad and my only living grandparent. But he was still my favourite.

"I'm going to get there first. I'm going to get there first," I whispered into my red wool scarf, double-wrapped over my mouth, as I trudged down Walker Road. It must have been minus 15 that morning, but I didn't care. I was on a mission. By the time I rounded the corner, my scarf was damp from the moisture of my breath and my constant chant. In the distance, I heard a dog barking. A moment later, out of the corner of my eye, I saw a furry grey bundle leap from the bushes and land on the street. I stopped in my tracks. The rabbit stopped too. It turned toward me and sat there for a few moments in the glow of the light coming from the houses on either side of the street. The rabbit cocked its head and its nose twitched, making its whiskers dance. It sat up on its hind legs and waved its paw as though it were wishing me a Happy New Year. Then a sudden blast of wind stirred up the freshly fallen snow, causing it to swirl up around the rabbit, and when it settled once more, the rabbit had disappeared.

I gaped for a moment. Where had the rabbit gone? Strange, it reminded me of the rabbit from my hunting trip with Grampy. The biting wind kicked up again, and I snapped out of my reverie and hurried along. I couldn't wait to see the look on Grampy's face when I got to his house.

The silver pocket watch gleamed in my mind's eye. No one else had been on the road. My brothers were fast asleep. They didn't care. Not like I did. I was bound and determined to be the one. I wanted that watch.

Grampy had announced to us kids on Christmas Day that he would give the watch to whoever arrived first at his house on New Year's Day. He told my cousins the same thing too. "I hope I'm first. I hope I'm first." I mumbled, clunking up the steps to Grampy's house across the street from Gerry's.

I thumped on the front door, my hand encased in two pairs of mittens. A few moments later, the door opened to reveal Grampy's grizzled grin.

"Happy New Year, Grampy!" My voice was muffled by the scarf.

"Damn, it's cold enough to freeze yer balls!" Grampy's booming laugh echoed around us, and he ushered me in to the small house. After Grampy sold the nun's house to my mom and dad, he bought a trailer and lived in our backyard, but when he got married again, his new wife declared that he'd better get a house for them to live in because there was no way she was going to piss in a bucket in a trailer.

"Did ye have yer breakfast yet, Timmy?"

"No, Grampy, I wanted to get here as soon as I could."

"Well, take off those heavy clothes and come into the kitchen. Grammy Lola is still asleep, so keep your voice down. She had a bit too much champagne last night and needs a little extra beauty sleep."

Grammy Lola was Grampy's third wife. I wondered what all the Grammys talked about in Heaven. Maybe they all smiled and shared funny stories about how Grampy always farted at the kitchen table and then said it was the dog, even though he didn't have a dog.

My grandfather padded down the short hallway into the kitchen. I yanked off my layers and laid them on the floor around wood stove in the small sitting room to warm up for when I had to head home. Then I scurried down the hall and stepped into the kitchen as Grampy was cracking two eggs in a skillet. He lifted the lid of the white enamel bread box, pulled out a loaf of dark bread and set it on a wooden cutting board. Sliding a large serrated knife into the loaf, he cut off two thick slices and slipped them into the pre-heated oven.

Grampy set a cup of hot apple cider in front of me as I pulled out one of the kitchen chairs at the table, covered in a Christmas-green vinyl table cloth. "Have a sip of that, Timmy. It'll warm you up."

I picked up the cup and took a drink. Sweet and tart, it warmed me from my toes to my head.

Grampy never drank beer or alcohol in front of us kids. Mum and Dad did, especially on weekends and holidays. But I don't think I ever saw Grampy take a drop of anything. Maybe by the time I was born, Grampy had left his drinking days behind him. For some odd reason, it made me happy that Grampy didn't drink.

I took another sip of cider as Grampy set a plate in front of me with a slice of thick toast spread with margarine and a sunny-side up fried egg, then gave me a glass of milk. I dug in, breaking off a chunk of the toasted bread and dipping it into the gooey, golden yolk on my plate and slurping it up.

"I'm glad you showed up this morning, Timmy," Grampy said around a mouthful egg. "I had a feeling you'd be the first one here."

"You did?" I asked, "How come?"

"Because you wanted it the most."

"But how did you know that?"

"Because I know you, Timmy. You might not be the tallest, or the strongest, or the biggest, but you work the hardest. When you want something, you figure out a way to get it."

Grampy's words sunk in. Was that what made me different from my brothers and cousins? Was it because I worked the hardest? I thought back to winning the David Sears Trophy. My best friend Sammy Roth was a better athlete than me. He made everything look so easy. But I knew nothing was easy. I knew life wasn't easy. That's why I worked so hard for what I wanted.

"What time is it, Grampy?" I asked, my voice laced with excitement.

"Well, now let me check *your* watch." Grampy chuckled again as he pulled the watch out from his pocket and glanced at it. "It's six thirty," he said. "Tim, I'm going to tell you about this watch before I show you how to work it."

I sat wide-eyed as Grampy told me about the day his dad gave him the watch.

"My father," he began, "your great-grandfather, gifted me this watch when I was about your age. The watch belonged to *his* father, who was your great-great grandfather."

"Wow!"

Grampy winked at me. "This watch has a secret."

"What kind of secret?" I was so eager to find out, I was kicking my chair.

Grampy crooked his finger at me, and I got up from my chair and walked to his side. The old man turned over the watch so I could read the initials on the back. *DLB.*

The initials were intricately carved and reminded me of the handwriting guides my teacher had posted above the blackboard at school to show us proper penmanship. Reaching out, I tentatively traced the D with my index finger, then the L and the B, feeling the delicate groove of the letters.

"He engraved it just for you," I said.

"No, he didn't." Grampy must have read the confusion on my face because he laughed and mussed my hair. "When I was born, my father, Anselme LeBlanc named me Dosite LeBlanc after *his* father, Dosithe LeBlanc. Same initials except I don't have the "h" in my name.

"Grampy, everyone calls you Dos."

"Yeah, that's my nickname," he said with a smile. "But my given name is actually Dosite, which was my grandfather's name.

"So, when your dad gave you the watch, it was like it was made just for you because the initials on the back match your name, right?" I jumped up and down. "Can I hold it, Grampy?"

"Hold out your hand Timmy."

I wiped my hand on my sweater and held it out.

His eyes glowed with warmth as he set the watch in the palm of my hand.

"And now it belongs to you."

Grampy must have polished it the night before,

because it gleamed. Grampy pointed out all the parts of the watch to me, including the knob on the top and the chain attached to the knob that hooked into your pocket. The hands had a tip that looked a bit like the fleur-de-lis.

I gazed at the watch for a long time. It felt heavy in my hand. Like it was telling me its worth; whispering its secrets to me. It had belonged to my great-great grandfather and then to my great-grandfather and then to my grandfather—and now it belonged to me.

"Look at this watch," Grampy told me. "Look at the second hand moving around the dial. Do you feel it ticking in your hand?"

"Yes, Grampy." I said with reverence.

"That ticking matches the beat in our hearts. It reminds us that we're alive. That we have a life to live. Time is like money; we have to spend it wisely or we'll end up waking up one day and realize we've squandered all of it." Grampy wrapped his arm around my shoulders and gave me a hug. "I know you're going to be successful in your life, just as I knew you'd be the one to show up here on my doorstep this morning. You want it. And you're willing to work hard to get it."

Grampy's words echoed in my ears as I walked home an hour later, the watch snuggled against my palm inside my double pair of mittens: *"I knew you'd be the one to show up here on my doorstep this morning."* I had wanted the watch more than my brothers and cousins. I'd wanted it so much that I got up before dawn on New Year's Day and trudged through the cold. I wanted it because it was Grampy's. It was special. It meant something to him, and it meant something to me too. I wanted it, and I worked hard to get it.

My brothers and cousins may have wanted the watch in a fleeting moment. They would have accepted the watch if it had just been handed over to them. But they didn't want it badly enough to work for it. They preferred to sleep in and stay warm and snug under their blankets.

Looking back, I learned a valuable lesson that day. You can want something, but if you aren't willing to put in the time and work it takes to get it, then you might as well just roll over and go back to bed.

There is a difference between wanting something and wanting to work for something. There is a difference between saying you want to change and actually doing the work every day to make it happen. That's what it means to Own Your Shit. It's about doing, not wanting. When you Own Your Shit, you are making a commitment to work for something you want. Anyone can want to lose weight, or stop smoking, or quit drinking or be a better partner or parent, but if you're not willing to put in the time to work for it, then you are metaphorically just rolling over in your bed.

The stories in this book, from my childhood, are meant to make you think about your life, your own childhood. What did you learn growing up that truly resonated with you? Have you forgotten your own life lessons because of the passage of time? I want you to remember them.

Think back to your own childhood. Think about a lesson that you learned from spending time with an elder in your family—a parent, grandparent, aunt/

uncle—or perhaps a coach or a teacher or neighbour. Take a few minutes to write about it. What do you remember about that memory? Why did it make a big impact on you? Looking back, what did you learn about yourself and what's important in life?

I cherished that watch for many years until I lost it on a trip out west. To this day, it saddens me that I no longer have that physical connection to my grandfather and my grandfathers before him. But I still have my memories. And more importantly, I cherish those memories of spending time with Grampy. I cherish all the things he taught me about trapping, hunting, and fishing. Lessons about life. Lessons about working hard for something you really want.

Chapter 10

Make Spiritual Reflection Part of Your Everyday Life.

"How people treat you is their karma;
how you react is yours."
— *Wayne W. Dyer*

I was plunged into darkness. I turned in a slow circle searching for a ray of light, but all I could see in front of me was black earth. Worms poked through the crumbled layers of the moist, heavy soil around me. Some were whole, while others were severed, victims of the sharp edge of my shovel. I shivered as I stabbed at the dirt and flung one last clump up and over my head.

This was it. The end. No going back. Not for this fella.

There is no other way to explain grave digging.

You are literally standing in death.

You are a stand-in.

You are standing in the place where a dead person will reside for eternity.

But you were there first.

"You okay down there, Timmy?" Dad's voice

floated down to me. He sounded far away, but he was standing only a few feet above me.

"Yeah, Dad," I squeaked.

"Well, come on up and have something to eat." He reached down to help me climb out of the grave and I grabbed his hand like a lifeline.

When I was a kid, my dad and I made part-time money digging graves for Middle Sackville Catholic Cemetery. My Uncle Roy got the contract for the job, but being small and limber, I was the one stuck hopping into the hole. Believe me, it's not a feeling I will ever forget. I am still haunted by that feeling of suffocation that comes with standing in an open grave—and I can't quite believe that I dug graves as a kid.

"There you go," Uncle Roy chuckled and slapped me on the back. "You're a tough kid, Timmy." He handed me a tuna sandwich, and I took it gratefully. As I took my first bite, I closed my eyes. It was the best sandwich I had ever tasted. I didn't know why it tasted to so good, but it did.

I finished my sandwich and sat on a stump while Uncle Roy and Dad swapped funny stories from their childhoods. Their laughter made me smile. I turned my face up to the sun. Its warmth felt like a hug from God. A few minutes ago, I had been in the suffocating dark, and now I was in the glow of a bright day. Why had I been so scared? I wasn't dead. And even if I were dead, I wouldn't have cause to be scared, because I'd be dead.

As an altar boy, I saw the highest highs and the lowest lows. I observed the brightest joy and the deepest despair. I witnessed the beginning and the end of people's lives. In the five or so years I served, I must have assisted in hundreds of special masses from baptisms to first communions to confirmations to weddings and yes, funerals. It's a lot to take in when you're a kid.

But if there is one job where you really can take stock of who you are and where you're going—it's digging graves.

On the bright side, the dead can't bully you. They can't call you names or make fun of your hand-me-down clothes. But when you're in that dark hole, there is a quiet solitude that surrounds you that comes with standing so close to death.

I've changed in many ways over the last ten years. But every day, I've continued to embrace life and seek new challenges, and to Own My Shit. I've also taken time for spiritual reflection, and I believe I am a far more spiritual person today than I was ten years ago.

I often wonder why we're so afraid of dying. Yes, it's the "great unknown," but maybe fear of death is really just the fear of not having lived enough before we die. At least not the kind of lives we want to live. I don't mean in the sense of quitting your job and moving to a Greek Island—not that there's anything wrong with that—I mean being present in your own skin. Taking a moment to smile and enjoy the sun on your face.

The sunshine is waiting for you right outside your front door. It's the exact same sun you'd find on that Greek Island. It belongs to all of us, so enjoy it.

There are many paths to spiritual balance, and everyone has their own way of getting there. And I believe that no matter what your religious beliefs are, your spirituality is as unique and individual as a snowflake. Everyone is different.

You could be at the end of your life right now, and not even know it. You could step off the curb and be hit by a truck. The question I ask you is this: have you lived a good life? Are you happy in your soul? You can't measure happiness in terms of money. You might be able to afford a swanky casket made of gold, but it won't do a thing for you in the Great Unknown.

And being able to afford a gold casket doesn't mean people will show up at your funeral.

I remember reading somewhere, "If you had to sit down and write your own eulogy, what would you say? Would you talk about all the money you made in your lifetime?" No, of course not. You would talk about your family and friends. You would have a special message for each of them. You would tell them how much you love them. You might mention some notable accomplishments when it comes to career achievement, such as starting your own company and running it for 25 years. You might mention that every employee was like a member of your family, and your favourite thing to do was to surprise them on their birthday with a cake and to sing Happy Birthday to them. You might mention that you coached a kids' soccer team and how the team effort meant more than the wins. You might share a story about your final days in hospice, and how kind everyone was, but what you loved even more were the practical jokes the nurses played on each other.

Religion teaches us to have faith in the unknown. Humanity teaches us to have faith in each other. And there is nothing "unknown" or "unseen" about that. When you reach out to someone in need, when you help someone, when you do a kindness for someone, it makes you feel good, doesn't it? Why does it feel good? Because you are making a difference in someone else's life. And by doing that, you are enriching your own.

You might ask what does Owning Your Shit have to do with Spirituality? The answer is, a lot. Owning Your Shit is about taking responsibility for your life and your actions, yes, but you don't live in a bubble, either. Being responsible means thinking beyond yourself. Caring about others beyond yourself. Respecting the world beyond yourself.

Owning Your Shit means being honest with yourself and with everyone in your life. It means being authentic in your life. It means living your life with integrity. And if we forget and stumble, we need to own that too. There are three magic words that will always put you back on the right path. I. Am. Sorry.

The truth is the inner echo of what we know to be right and just. This is the path we are on. This is the road we travel every day.

Every day the traffic on my way to work is bumper to bumper. And every day we all wait to make that left turn. Unfortunately, there's also that one person who thinks they can jump the line. They drive in the righthand lane as though they are going straight through, but when they get to the intersection, they suddenly make a quick left and jump ahead of everyone else who was waiting their turn.

I'd witnessed this happen several times, and I had had enough. I followed the guy who did it, and when he reached the next intersection, I pulled up beside him and gestured for him to roll down his window. I proceeded to yell at him for being selfish, stupid, and reckless, and for putting the rest of us at risk for a multi-vehicle crash because he didn't have his act together enough to get up a few minutes early and get into the left-turn lane like the rest of us.

The guy sat there, mouth agape, just staring at me. And then I saw them. A little boy and girl in the back seat. They stared at me too, their eyes as wide as saucers. I immediately apologized and went on my way. Here I was schooling this guy about Owning His Shit, when I failed to do it myself by yelling at the poor guy in front of his kids and probably scaring them too.

I knew where the guy lived. I didn't have to confront him like that. I could have just stopped off at his house and had a calm chat with him. I could have asked him if everything was okay, because I had seen him do that several times. I mean, who knows, maybe his wife was in the hospital and he had to do everything himself. I didn't know, and I hadn't bothered to find out. I just lashed out, and that's not what Owning Your Shit is about.

Owning Your Shit is about taking responsibility for your life and your actions—and that includes how you treat others. Spirituality is part of that. Don't lash out. Seek out.

As you reflect back on your life and the changes you want to make, take a moment to jot down a few instances where you lost your temper—maybe it was in line at the grocery store checkout, or at a restaurant with a waiter, or with another parent while you were dropping your kids off at school. Describe how you behaved. Did you apologize? Did you seek to make amends? How you would change your reaction the next time something like that happens?

If you choose to live your life always looking for a fight, then you'll always find one. If you choose to believe the world owes you something, then you will always feel cheated. If you believe you have the strength inside you to change, then you will. If you believe you can make a positive difference in someone's life, then you will.

Karma. I believe that what you put out in the world comes back to you. If all you have to offer the world is negativity, then negativity will always be around you. If you offer positivity, then you will be surrounded by the positive. Why? Because you have shifted your outlook. You have made a decision.

Make a decision to make a decision.

There are countless true stories of people who have overcome great odds to achieve great things. People who put out positive energy inspire us in a positive way. They instill in us the belief in the possible. And guess what? When you make a decision to make a decision, when you put positive energy out there and focus on your "possible," then you too will inspire someone else.

Try this. Make a list of positive things you've done or said. List the positive action in one column, and then write how you felt after doing or saying it in the other column.

The purpose of this simple exercise is to get you thinking about how doing something positive for someone else impacts you. Does this mean we should allow people to walk all over us? No, of course not. Part of Owning Your Shit is being honest and forthright. If you have to speak up and address an issue or a problem, then that is a responsible thing to do.

Chapter 11

Focus on the Right Reasons for Success, Not the Wrong Ones.

"Sometimes you will never know the value of a moment, until it becomes a memory."
— Dr. Seuss

I was the first one to get to Gerry's store. My older brother Kevin and my younger brother Rob were shuffling behind me. I shifted from foot to foot, impatient to get going. When the school bus arrived at a few minutes past 6:00 a.m., I flung my knapsack over my shoulder as I scrambled up the stairs and found an empty seat in the middle section of the bus. Mum had packed us each a cheese and bologna sandwich and a homemade cookie. I slid into the seat and Rob slipped in beside me. Kevin plopped himself down on the seat in front of us and stretched out. I sat with my knees close together, hoping no one would notice the tear in the inner seam of my bell-bottom pants. I forgot to ask Mum to sew it up. I hoped no one would notice.

About 20 minutes later, we arrived at the blueberry farm where the 30 or so kids would spend the day picking blueberries. I'd been doing this job every August since the age of twelve. I was the best blueberry picker in the area.

There were thirty rows of blueberries, each approximately two hundred yards long. In one hand we carried a bucket that could hold about five gallons, and in the other hand we carried a small rake shovel with a handle to sift through the bushes, so we could catch the blueberries as we moved along the row. We had to hunker down, kneel and crawl to get the berries because the bushes were low to the ground.

It was hot and we were itchy because of the bugs. We were fresh meat out there for all the flies and wasps and whatever else buzzed alongside us. It was inevitable. Around 2:00 p.m., the questions from my brothers would start. "Hey, Tim what bucket are you on?" Before I gave them my answer, I asked them what bucket they were on.

"I'm on bucket twelve," said Rob.

"I'm on bucket eleven," said Kevin.

"I'm on bucket forty-three," I said.

"How can you possibly be on bucket forty-three at two thirty in the afternoon?"

I grinned as I glanced at their blue-stained mouths. I knew that my brothers and the other kids ate their body weight in blueberries. I knew they'd stopped for an hour to eat their lunch and relax. I knew they took "breaks" and clustered in small groups to talk about who was dating whom and the upcoming school year.

I did none of those things.

Why?

Because I had something the other kids didn't have, including my brothers. You could call it an inner motivation or a drive. I didn't have a word for it back then. I didn't understand what it was. I only knew that I had this feeling inside me that was pushing me to keep going, keeping filling up pails even when I was hot, tired, and thirsty.

At two dollars a bucket, I quickly did the math in my head and knew that I could make 100 dollars in a day. Which, at that time in the 80s, was a big sum of money. But there was something else.

I was thinking about pants. Buying myself a brand new pair of pants. Something that I had never had before. But not just any pants. No, they had to be a designer brand. With the fancy name stitched on the back pocket.

"Hey, Timmy." Dennis Murphy, one of the older boys strutted up to me at the end of the day. "Hear you got the most pails today?" Two giggling girls hovered behind him. They'd spent most of the afternoon flirting and goofing off.

"Yeah, so what?" I replied with some bravado. I was younger and smaller than they were, but I was a pretty tough kid.

"What are you gonna do with all that money?"

"None of your beeswax," I answered, turning to pick up my knapsack.

"Maybe you can finally get yourself some nice duds." Dennis snickered as he and the two girls made a grab for my legs. They pushed me down on the ground and spread my legs, the seam tearing completely. Everyone around us, including the girls, could see my underwear.

They all laughed at me.

My brothers were on the other side of the field finishing up for the day. Too far away to help me.

I was on my own.

"Let me go!" I shouted, kicking out at them.

They raised their hands in mock surrender and stepped back. "Hey, no problem. We only wanted to congratulate you on being the best blueberry picker in town," Dennis said, and they all broke into laughter again.

I stood up and grabbed my bag, then made my way to the bus. I walked stiffly, because by now my pants were completely torn. The tears were streaming down my face. I wiped the back of my blueberry-stained hand across my cheeks.

Later, as the bus drove us home, I told my brothers what had happened. They wanted to beat the crap out of the bullies, but I told them no. I didn't want to start anything. It was better to let it go. Besides, I'd earned my 100 dollars, and I could finally buy those pants. My own clothes. Not hand-me-downs.

The best blueberry picker in town.

I would show them.

I would show all of them.

And I did.

I was never just picking blueberries. That's what the other kids were all doing, but not me. There was nothing fun about picking blueberries under a hot sun in the middle of summer while being bitten by bugs. But I got through it. I got through it because my mind went somewhere else. Somewhere far, far away. Today, looking back, my brothers and sisters don't understand where those feelings came from. They thought we had it pretty good.

I hated being bullied. I hated those hand-me-down pants. I hated having to live in an old, broken down nun's house with rats in the cellar. I hated that feeling of shame. Shame. I hated it with every fibre of my being. And I utilized that hatred as a driving force throughout my life. And that motivated me more than anything else. It went beyond money. It went beyond financial success. I was trying to run away from that little kid. The little kid who felt shame down to his bones and hated it.

Eventually, as I hit my stride in my career, that drive became my currency. It was what I used to propel myself ahead to achieve success. But I didn't *feel* successful. At least not deep down. In my gut, my core, my bones, I was still that kid with the torn bell-bottoms who hustled to fill the most blueberry pails.

One of the key lessons I learned when I began to Own My Shit is that if you are chasing a dream of success because of how others have treated you or because of a pain in your life or a rough childhood, then you will be forever chasing something. And you will never get there. No kind of success will ever be enough for you. Every achievement will feel hollow and empty.

Decades later, I figured out it wasn't about how many pails I could fill; it was about trying to fill what was missing in myself.

Chapter 12

The Truth and Nothing but the Truth. Always.

"Three things cannot be long hidden: the sun, the moon, and the truth."
— *Buddha*

Sometimes your dreams take you on a different road, so you'd better have a full tank of gas. But lies? Lies can only lead you to a dead end. I learned that firsthand. When I was 16 years old, my mom told me and Rob that we were taking a road trip. My older sister, Cathy, who was living out west, was flying home, and we would all drive out to Calgary to spend a few weeks with my oldest brother Greg.

Dad would be staying home with Kevin. Rob and I would be going with Mum and Cathy. Greg was married, and his wife was pregnant. Greg had enrolled me in hockey camp and had even bought me new skates. The idea was for me to see if I liked it there, and if I did, I could live with Greg and join a junior hockey league and maybe eventually I would be noticed by the NHL scouts.

"You've got some talent, Timmy," Dad said. "You're good enough for the NHL."

I was over the moon with excitement, although I wished Dad and Kevin were going too. But Kevin was older than me by two years and already had a summer job lined up and even a girlfriend. *Yuck,* was my reaction, of course.

But the truth has a funny way of punching you in the gut. After our first day on the road we checked into a motel for the night. It was pretty exciting since we'd rarely been so far from home that we needed to stay in a motel.

Robbie and I were lying on the faded floral bedspread on one of the double beds in the room and watching cartoons on TV, and Mum was unpacking our suitcase. Cathy came back, carrying a bucket of Kentucky Fried Chicken and a brown bag. Robbie and I let out a whoop and began to jump up and down on the bed. I couldn't remember the last time we had Kentucky Fried Chicken. I think it was a community picnic because Mum and Dad rarely splurged on restaurant food. Mum and Cathy filled our plates, and Robbie and I happily dug in. I bit into the crispy, salty skin and closed my eyes. It tasted like magic. If only Dad and Kevin were here, it would have been a real vacation.

And that's when Mum told us.

"Timmy. Robbie," she choked out, then took a sip of Pepsi. "I have to tell you kids something."

I set down the drumstick I held, sensing something was terribly wrong. I glanced at Rob, and his wide eyes reflected my own fear.

"We're not just going to Calgary for a visit," she said. "We're going for good."

"What about Dad and Kevin?" Robbie blurted out, his bottom lip trembling.

"Dad and Kevin will be staying back home," Cathy said in a soft voice.

"But that means we'll never see them again!" I cried out.

"Of course you'll see them," Mum said. Her voice sounded too wobbly. Her eyes were swimming with tears. I didn't believe her.

"Why are you doing this, Mum?" I asked in a broken voice. Why would she take us away from Dad and Kevin and our life?

"Because it's for the best," she replied. She took a deep breath and knelt on the carpet in front of us. Wrapping her arms around us she said in a muffled voice. "We're going to be happy. You just wait and see. Everything is going to be better. So much better."

Mom started to cry, and we were crying too. Cathy was crying. We were all crying.

It was the end. The end of my childhood, and I didn't even know it. I didn't even get a chance to say a proper goodbye.

I would never get to skate on Morice's Mill Pond again. I would never get to go hunting with Grampy again. I would never bike to Gerry's store to pick up a bag of milk for Mum. I would never see my friends again—Sammy Roth and Dennis and my cousins. Yes, Greg and Cathy and Frances had left home, but they were grown up when they left. Kevin and I were just kids.

And what about Dad? How would he manage without us? At least he still had Kevin. That didn't make me feel any better.

Everything had changed. Nothing would ever be the same again. Mum was leaving Dad and we were moving out west to live with Greg for a while until Mum could find us a place. Greg actually did buy me new skates and he did want me to play hockey. But that wasn't the point. Rob and I were heartbroken and angry that our mother had lied to us. Heck, everyone had lied to us because they thought we were too young to understand. They'd made all of these "adult" decisions without talking to us.

Mum and Dad had always had problems, and there was many a fight in our house over the years, mostly due to money (or lack thereof), but as a kid you don't think about the D-word when it comes to your parents. My parents had been together for almost 30 years, and that was forever to me.

But Mum had made a decision. And it impacted the entire family.

I suddenly found myself living in Calgary, Alberta from the age of 16 onward. I did play hockey for a few years, but I eventually realized that I was no match for many of the players in the other youth leagues. Back home, I was a big fish skating on a small pond. But in Calgary, I was just another kid who played pretty good but would never be a Gordie Howe or a Wayne Gretzky or a Mario Lemieux. Calgary was and still is a big hockey town that has nurtured a lot of NHL talent over the years. Unfortunately, I wasn't one of them.

Between my parents' divorce, leaving my home town, and finding myself in a big city that lives and breathes hockey, I began to develop some serious behavioural issues in my teenage years. I became rebellious and skipped school on a regular basis. I indulged in underage drinking and smoking cigarettes, and I even tried some harder drugs. Eventually, I dropped out of high school and started working with Greg at Wasea Metal where he was the manager.

Looking back, those years of transition were rough, as they would be for any kid in my position. I missed all of us just sitting around the dinner table listening to my dad's stories, seeing who could gobble up the stew the fastest and get seconds. I missed my friends and Kevin, and I missed Dad. But most of all I missed home.

Greg was more like a second father to me than a big brother. I will never forget how much he believed in my ability to play hockey. But I was no longer a hockey star from Middle—Sackville, New Brunswick. I was Tim Richardson, just another teenager in a big city. I was no longer that kid who spent hours at Morice's Old Mill Pond gliding on the ice, shifting the puck from left to right as he dreamed of playing in the NHL.

I was broken inside, and I didn't know how to fix myself.

I was broken because of the move and my parents' divorce. But most of all, I was broken because of the lies my mother told me.

One of the most important foundations of Owning Your Shit is to tell the truth. Live a truthful life. Be open and honest in all things, even when it's difficult. My mother and father had not been honest about their divorce, and that had a big impact on me.

Don't think that lies make things easier. They

don't. Lies have a way of building up to the point where you have created a huge wall between you and your loved ones and the world around you. And when you do that, you can no longer see clearly.

Owning Your Shit means being honest with yourself and others. Even if it hurts you and them. At the end of the day, you are showing that person the respect they deserve by being honest with them.

Chapter 13

Your Mentors Are Out There, You Just Have to Open Your Mind.

"Opportunities are usually disguised as hard work, so most people don't recognize them."
— Ann Landers

It was a bright, sunny day in May. The sky was a crystal, clear blue, but there was still a bite in the air that is typical of spring time in Calgary. I parked my truck in the parking lot behind a sprawling building that resembled a California Ranch and Spa surrounded by miles of emerald green grass instead of desert. Beyond that lay a border of trees. I got out of my truck and made my way into the main office of the Douglasdale Estates Golf Club. The man I needed to speak to was the manager, Chuck Shields.

I was a high school dropout who'd stumbled into a brief detour into drugs. That inner fire that had been burning inside me ever since I was a little kid had fizzled out in my teen years. I'd travelled a rocky road from Middle Sackville, New Brunswick to Calgary, Alberta and ended up working for a company that produced sheet metal.

But somewhere, deep down inside me, was a small ember. A spark. I had to reignite that spark into a flame. Then the idea hit me.

I may have lost my chance at the NHL, but there was still golf.

"If you're looking for a job in the kitchen, you need to go downstairs," the middle-aged man said, barely glancing in my direction. He sat behind an oak desk, half-glasses perched on the end of his nose as he flipped through a neatly stacked pile of file folders.

"Actually, I'm here to apply for a job as golf pro," I replied.

The man glanced up, and his gaze scanned me up and down. I don't know what he saw that day in an 18-year-old, lanky kid with long, shaggy hair wearing a leather jacket, jeans and cowboy boots, but I'll give Chuck credit. He didn't toss me out on my ass, as anyone else in his shoes might have done. No, instead Chuck leaned back in his swivel chair and gave me a hard look over the rim of his glasses. He must have seen beyond that cocky-looking young man to the scared kid underneath. He must have seen the desperate hope in my eyes because the next words out of his mouth changed the trajectory of my life.

"Son, I can't hire you on as a golf pro because I don't know how well you play. Tell you what. I'm going to give you the back shop. You're going to clean the members' clubs and all the motorized golf carts—the rentals, the pull carts, all of that. And you'll prep the range. I'll give you a staff of eight kids between the ages of twelve and sixteen to help you. If you can manage them and do a good job with the other chores, you can golf in the summer, and I'll watch you play. See what you've got to offer. Deal?"

"Deal!" I replied. I was thrilled. "Thank you, Mr. Shields. I appreciate your faith in me."

"You can call me Chuck," he said with a smile.

"Yes, sir, Mr. Shields."

He laughed as he stood up and gestured for me to follow him.

"Son, the first order of business is about your clothes. No jeans and leather jacket and cowboy boots."

He glanced up and down at me again with a raised eyebrow.

"Yes, Mr. Shields," I replied, as I realized my mistake. Chuck was dressed in a crisp polo shirt, monogrammed with the Douglasdale logo and pressed navy slacks. On his feet were a pair of brown loafers.

On the tour of the grounds, he took me to the kitchen from the back way. He glanced into the garbage Dumpster behind the building. Chuck picked up a stool, set it down beside the Dumpster, stepped up to its rim, and proceeded to climb in as I watched, wondering what he'd seen. A dead animal? A wallet? A gold watch that belonged to one of the members?

"Tim, can you give me a hand?"

"Yes sir." I stepped up onto the stool. Looking down into the Dumpster, I was surprised by what Chuck was doing.

He was picking up empty beer bottles.

He turned and began handing them to me.

"Set those down by the back door of the kitchen for me."

"Yes, Mr. Shields."

"Call me Chuck."

"Yes, Mr. Shields."

"You know, Tim, the staff likes to have a beer out here in the back, and that's fine, but we need to return the empties to the beer store, so we can get the bottle deposit. That's revenue, and it adds up. Every little bit counts." he said with a wink.

"I understand, Mr. Shields."

"Call me Chuck."

"Yes, Mr. Shields."

It took seven more times of Chuck telling me I could call him Chuck before I actually did.

We have mentors throughout our lives. People who share wisdom not necessarily in words but in deeds. Chuck could have asked me to hop in the Dumpster to retrieve the beer bottles. After all, I was the kid, and I was dressed in jeans, not in a suit. But he didn't. He did it himself, and he took the time to explain to me why it was important.

No job is too big or small.

Chuck cared about the business he was managing. He had respect for all the parts that kept it running. When he jumped in that Dumpster, he showed me that he didn't put himself above me. Chuck didn't have himself up on a pedestal. It didn't matter that he was the boss and I was the lowly, newly hired employee. He Owned His Shit.

That was an important lesson for me.

Today, I operate in the same way. I am part of a team. I am not the "boss". Even though I'm a Regional Director, I operate as a team member. Everyone's role is important and valuable. Everyone contributes to the success of an organization.

Chuck became a true mentor for me over the years. He still is a mentor and a dear friend.

Think back to your childhood, teen years, early

20s, 30s, or even the past few years. Who have you met along the way that really made an impact? How did they make an impact?

As you travel on your journey, think about the kind of mentor you want to be. It doesn't have to be in a work setting. It could be as a volunteer, or even to a friend or neighbour. Think about the positive impact you can have on someone else's life. Write it down. Make it a goal.

Chapter 14

Respect the World Around You and Lead by Example and Action, Not by Negativity and Complaint.

There is no respect for others without humility in one's self.
— Henri Frédéric Amiel

Boy, was I tired. I had just completed the final leg of a four-city tour that involved wall-to-wall meetings and presentations. My work takes me all over Canada and the United States. I love what I do, and I love making a difference in people's lives. I love to inspire and motivate our teams to work better together and to become stronger and more productive.

A few years ago, after I began my own personal journey and improved my health and my outlook, I pondered the idea of bringing the Own Your Shit philosophy into my presentations with the professionals that I met across North America.

The changes that had impacted my life were tremendous. When I began to Own My Shit, my excess weight came off, I was able to stick to a smoke-free life, I began to work out every day, and I was no longer eating fast food at my desk or over-indulging in high fat and high sugar foods. My sleep began to improve, my mood brightened, and my relationships with my loved ones and friends and colleagues transformed for the better. Best of all, my overall outlook on life had shifted. It was no longer about me. It was no longer about how much money I could make or how successful I could be. Instead, I began to think about how I could help others. What kind of impact could I make on other people's lives? I mean beyond sales. Beyond work.

I began to think about how I could impact people's lives for the better. I reflected back on my own life, my childhood, and the hard knocks that I experienced growing up—and how I was able to right all the wrongs I had committed. Maybe, I thought, I could begin to share some of my childhood experiences and some of the life lessons I've learned over the years. So, I did. I began to share my story, and you know what? It resonated with the people I met. I felt heartened by the feedback I got at my presentations.

But at end of that particular four-city tour, I was on the flight home and something happened. About an hour after takeoff, I got up to use the bathroom. Now, if you've ever been on a plane, you know those toilets are tiny and don't exactly offer the comforts of home. But when I stepped into the bathroom, my eyes widened at what I saw. Urine. All over the seat and the floor. Since holding it in wasn't an option for me, I did what had to be done. I Owned My Shit. Or rather, held my piss.

I grabbed a wad of paper towels, dampened them in water and pumped some liquid soap into the make-do sponge and proceeded to do a cleanup job, wiping down the toilet first, then grabbing another damp, soapy wad of towels and mopping up the floor. After drying everything, I proceeded to wash my hands and take care of my business. And I used some hand sanitizer to wipe the door handle for good measure.

As I returned to my seat, I couldn't help but feel disgusted at the person or persons who left the toilet like a pig sty. I also wondered why everyone who'd stepped in there before me had just ignored the mess or contributed to it. How can you have any self-respect and behave in such a manner? I realize you can't clean every restroom in every subway station, shopping mall, or sports stadium—and I'm not saying you should go find a mop and bucket and clean the entire bathroom. Yes, people get paid to clean bathrooms in public spaces. Yes, if you're in a hurry and have to catch your subway, you can't stop and clean. Yes, I know all the arguments. But if everyone had self-respect, we wouldn't create these circumstances in the first place. We wouldn't walk into a public washroom and find ourselves standing in a puddle of urine.

In my particular situation, I made a call, and it was the right one. I could have just done what the person ahead of me had done and just ignored it. Even if I hadn't caused the mess, I had to be the one to clean it up. Why did I clean It up? Because I have self-respect. Because I have respect for others. Because I Own My Shit.

I took a sip from my water bottle, wondering if my entire philosophy of Owning Your Shit was just me whistling in the wind. Did it matter? Was I truly making a difference? Was it worth the trouble? Or was I just wasting my time and efforts?

A few moments later, an elderly lady with a cane walked past me and stepped into the bathroom.

I closed my eyes and released a deep breath.

The universe had just sent me an answer.

That little old lady walked into a clean bathroom. She was able to sit on a clean toilet seat. Without knowing it, I made it possible for a little old lady to go to the bathroom with comfort because I Owned My Shit.

Are you going to be someone who sits in piss or who cleans it up?

Eight years ago, I decided I would no longer accept anything but the highest standard from myself. And I haven't stopped since.

What does that mean? It means having as much respect for everything around you as you do for yourself because we are all connected. Because that old woman was someone's mother and grandmother. She could have been my grandmother or yours. Every person should live with dignity. If you treat others with respect and kindness, it will come back to you tenfold. You may not see it, you may not even know it, but it's there.

Even if I hadn't seen the elderly woman with the cane, all I had to do was think about the next person who used that bathroom. This is at the heart of what it means to Own Your Shit. You don't need to know who will go into the bathroom you cleaned up; all you have to know is that you left it cleaner than when you went in.

Isn't that a metaphor for life?

Owning Your Shit means taking responsibility for yourself even if that means cleaning up someone else's mess. Because when you encounter that mess, and you turn a blind eye, then you become part of it.

Do you want to go through life being part of the problem or part of the solution?

Owning Your Shit means making the world around you a better place, even if that means wiping down the toilet.

Every day there are videos on the internet of people saying and doing nasty stuff in grocery stores, parking lots, coffee shops. Every day there are people being rude, crude, and spreading misery around. Whether or not you get captured on video, ask yourself: Are you like those people? Do you want to be?

I'm not telling you to be Mr. or Ms. Sunshine every day of your life. Nor am I telling you that you can't ever have a bad day or ever have an argument.

What I am telling you is that if something feels wrong in your gut, then it probably is. Sometimes it's as obvious as piss on a toilet. Other times, it's not. Just listen to that inner echo. Listen to your inner Gazoo. Pay attention to the world around you, big and small.

I was at my local golf course a few weeks ago, and I saw empty sandwich bags strewn on the green. Obviously, a group of golfing buddies had had a snack while they were playing. I picked them up and pocketed them. When I got back to the clubhouse, I threw them in the garbage bin. No biggie. I do that a lot. I Own My Shit and that includes picking up garbage.

But let me tell you what those golfing buddies really did.

By not pocketing their sandwich wrappers and

throwing them out at the clubhouse after their game, they made a very clear decision to pollute. They made a decision to be lazy and not care about their surroundings. They made a decision to not care about the next group of golfers coming after them. And they made a decision that their comfort was more important than anyone else's, so why bother going out of their way hang onto the plastic baggies until they got to a garbage bin? That's what the membership fees are for, right? To pay for the staff to pick up after the members. Who cares, right?

Wrong!

Why not just pocket the empty sandwich bags and then toss them in a garbage can later? The answer to that question is because they did not Own Their Shit. Just like the people on the plane who left urine on the toilet seat and the floor. Instead of Owning Their Shit, they didn't *give* a shit. That is unacceptable to me. And I hope it's unacceptable to you. Or that it will be after you're finished reading this book.

Most of us believe we're good people. But have you ever stopped to really think about what your values are? How do you define them? If you look up "values" in a dictionary, you'll most likely see the following words:

Attitude
Character
Code
Conduct
Conscience
Ethics
Integrity
Morals

Mores
Personal Beliefs
Scruples
Worth

I'm sure you can think of many more words that describe values. But what about the actions that go with the words?

Here's a simple exercise: I want you to write a list in two columns. You can create it on your computer, or use a sheet of paper, or a notebook. In the first column, I want you to list all your values. What is most important to you? In the second column, I want you to list your desires and dreams. They can be as big or as small as you want. The lists can be long or short. It's up to you.

The purpose of this simple exercise is for you to figure out the difference between *who you are* and *what you want*. Who you are, or your values, is not the same as what you want, or your goals.

Your values reflect who you are as a significant other/spouse, parent/guardian, employer/employee, son/daughter, friend, person, citizen, human being. Your values reflect how you behave in any given situation.

Your goals, on the other hand, are what you want to achieve in life. Your dreams and desires, both internal and external.

The way you align those two lists—the way you reconcile them and live your values (who you are) while working towards your goals (what you want)— is by Owning Your Shit.

Chapter 15

Change Can Only Happen When
You Own Your Shit.

*"It's not about perfect. It's about effort.
And when you bring that effort every single day,
that's where transformation happens.
That's how change occurs."*
— *Jillian Michaels*

Last year, my wife Annie suggested we try a 21-day no sugar/no carb reboot. I asked if she was absolutely sure because once I say yes and commit to something, that's it, there's no going back.

I Own My Shit and I never negotiate with myself.

I checked my calendar to make sure I wasn't going to be travelling anywhere that month. I admit, it's a challenge to stay on a new plan when I travel. It's doable, but why put that kind of stress on yourself? Not to mention, doing a weight loss or detox or reboot program with a friend or loved one makes it more challenging for them if you are off the grid for a few days.

My reboot challenge with Annie was a go! My calendar was clear, no travelling for a while, so we had time to do this right. We did our shopping that Saturday and stocked up the pantry and fridge with plenty of fresh veggies, chicken, fish, sparkling water, lemons and limes. On Sunday, we hopped online and found some fun new recipes we could try as we planned our meals for the week.

The first few days were a breeze. We were both on track. We left colourful sticky notes around the house with encouraging quotes. We made sure to have dinner together at the same time, and we cleaned up and made sure to prep everything for the next day.

Then day four arrived. Cue the suspense music. I came home after my workout and made my way to Annie's office, where she was working on setting up a viewing schedule for her clients. Annie is a real estate agent and works from home. As I stepped into her office, my mouth dropped open. Sitting on the desk beside her laptop was a McDonald's bag. The aroma of French fries wafted over to greet me.

"Hey, what happened to our twenty-one-day reboot?" I asked her.

"Oh, give me a break, I had a stressful day," she replied with an eyeroll. "Live a little, Tim. You can take the night off too. We'll start back up tomorrow."

"Nope," I said. "I committed to this reboot, and that's what I'm going to keep doing."

I strolled into the bedroom to grab a shower, but before I did, I texted her with *#ownyourshit.*

I won't tell you what she texted back, suffice it to say it contained another # with some choice four-letter words attached. Now, keep in mind that Annie and I love to joke with each other, and we support each other every day. I understood she'd had a stressful day and that she reacted to that stress with a need to comfort herself with food. But when we eat to seek comfort instead of eating to fuel our bodies, then we're forever running on empty.

Think about that.

When we eat to seek comfort instead of eating to fuel our bodies, we're forever running on empty.

When you use food (or smoking or drinking) as a way to cope with emotional issues in your life, or to assuage yourself when you're angry or upset, or to relax when your stress is in overdrive, or to get a burst of happiness when you're feeling low—then you have a problem.

When we abuse food, it's never about the actual food. I have never met anyone who is 100 pounds overweight because they love food. Most people who have a weight issue are that way because of what's going on in their heads. And that has to do with negative emotions that manifest in negative actions. Similarly, when we smoke or drink to excess, it's never about the "what," it's always about the "why."

I couldn't lose my excess weight until I figured out why I got fat in the first place. Part of that soul searching I did in 2012 was to figure that out. Growing up working class poor in a small town, we always had enough to eat but rarely had money left over for extravagances like takeout food. Our version of "takeout" was carrying the food from the stove to the dinner table. We learned to eat fast, because that meant you could get seconds.

And as I previously mentioned, we had a garden on a hilltop behind our house, and most of our meals were homemade. We were physically active. We walked everywhere, rode our bikes, and skated on

Morice's Mill Pond in winter. I played hockey in the winter and golf in the summer. And we worked every summer picking blueberries for local farmers and doing odd jobs. Our days were full of physical activity. We were lean and strong, and we ate very little junk food.

The McDonald's Happy Meal I got with my team mates after our hockey games was the extent of my fast food consumption. It wasn't until I was in my early 30s that I began to put on weight. I was living in Calgary by then and building my financial planning practice. Fast food, takeout, and a sedentary lifestyle became my norm. I tried numerous times to lose those extra pounds, but I always gained it back. Of course, it didn't help that I was also a heavy smoker and I drank. By the time I hit my 40s, I was more than 70 pounds overweight.

Both my parents smoked and drank in the house, in the car, in front of their children. Looking back, I know why they did it. It wasn't because they enjoyed it—although it did help to relax them—it was because they needed something to help take the edge off whatever they were feeling anxious about. And that was usually money. But as I found out, having money didn't take the edge off of my anxiety. I developed the same bad habits my parents had, and I didn't have poverty as a reason for my anxiety. My anxiety came from shame and lack of self-esteem, and that was difficult to overcome. Addiction is never about enjoyment. Addiction is both physical and psychological. The psychological/emotional part can be tough to figure out and even tougher to overcome. It's about avoiding the real issues, it's about numbing pain, it's about trying to forget what is eating away at you.

When food, alcohol, smoking, or drugs becomes your solace, it eventually turns into your burden.
So, I get it. I understand that it's not "just" about food. It's not that you love the taste of fries, although they do taste good. You're trying to feed yourself something that is missing from your life—and that may have been missing since you were a kid. I get why you keep those cigarettes hidden in that tea tin in the back of your cupboard. I understand why you have an extra glass of wine with dinner. You are self-medicating. You know that too. Deep down, you do. So, you have to find out what's going in your head. That might mean, reading, journaling, talking to a therapist. You need to figure out what some of the core negative emotions are that trigger you to eat in an unhealthy way, and you need to figure out what the situations are that can generate those emotions. Awareness is key.

What's important about health to you? What is your WHY?
What is your driving force? Do you want to be able to enjoy life after retirement? Do you want to be able to see your kids get married and to be an active grandparent? Do you have a parent or sibling who had issues with food, smoking, or drinking, or even drugs—and you know the toll it's taken on them? Have you lost a loved one due to an illness or accident that was related to smoking, drinking, drugs, food? Or are you just tired of being tired all the time? Are you finally ready to shake those shackles of the past? You need to figure out what your WHY is and you need to keep it front and centre every day.

But the "why" is only part of it. You also need the follow-through. The commitment. I tried in the past to quit smoking, ease back on my drinking, eat healthy and exercise—but I would eventually stumble and fall. Was it important to me? Yes. But if it was so important, why did I fail? I had my "why," didn't I?

Then it hit me. I wasn't Owning My Shit.

It wasn't until I began to Own My Shit that I lost the excess weight, gave up drinking, quit smoking, and included exercise in my daily routine. I am now the healthiest I've ever been.

And you know what? I worked damn hard to get there. It wasn't easy. I quit everything cold turkey. It took effort, time, and commitment. I cut out all the "white stuff," meaning sugar and white flour baked goods. I went to the gym every day. I drank two litres of water every day. I threw out the cigarettes. I stopped drinking.

There are tons of programs and apps and books and websites that can help you with all the details of what you need to do. There are experts who can help you with the steps you need to take to make a significant healthy shift in your life.

But at the end of the day, it comes down to you. It comes down to Owning Your Shit.

Take responsibility for everything you eat, smoke, and drink. Take responsibility when you don't go to the gym or for that walk or that swim. Don't blame someone else. Don't use the "work" excuse or "too many family obligations." And finally, don't negotiate with yourself. Don't give yourself an "out."

Stack the deck in your favour

When I share my story with people, I sometimes get the *why should I bother* response. "What if I go to the gym every day for two hours and eat sprouts and I still get a brain tumor or get hit by a car? Why should I bother?"

"Stack the deck in your favour," I reply.

There are 52 cards in a deck. In that deck, 26 are black and 26 are red. Let's say black represents negative health and red is positive. If I were to ask you to pull a card from the deck, there's a 50 per cent chance that you might pull a black card. But what if you take a 30-minute walk every day? Well, that's six less black cards in the deck. And what if you ordered the salad with grilled chicken instead of the bacon carbonara on Wednesday nights at your favourite restaurant? *Whoosh!* There go another three black cards up in smoke. What if you got a solid eight hours sleep at night instead of your usual six? Aha! Six more black cards have disappeared. What if you drank eight glasses of filtered water a day instead of pop, coffee, and beer? Well, there go another three black cards. So now, you're left with eight black cards in the deck and 26 red cards. Your chances of pulling a black card have gone way down.

You've just stacked the deck in your favour.

And if you do pull a black card, you will be stronger, healthier, and more determined to fight whatever comes your way.

Take the time to make the time.

You—and only you—are responsible.

When we were babies, our parents decided what we ate. But that changed from the moment you grabbed that box of corn flakes, shook it into a bowl, and poured in some milk. If you can make your own breakfast, you can and should decide what you put in your mouth.

One of the biggest hurdles to weight loss or quitting smoking or drinking is actually sticking to it. How many times have you started a new diet or quit smoking or drinking on January first? Yup, those good old-fashioned New Year's Resolutions. But a resolution is different than Owning Your Shit. As I said in Chapter 1, "make a decision to make a decision." When you decide to make a change, you must recommit to it every day. Making a resolution is easy. Keeping it means you're Owning Your Shit.

If you truly want to change, you need to give yourself the time to get used to that change.

Here are some tried and true tips that have worked for me:

1. Make the decision.
2. Recommit every single day. I carry laminated cards with me that are my daily affirmations. I read them every morning. Go online and find some inspiring quotes. Print them out on colour card stock and leave them all over the house as daily reminders for motivation.
3. Set up a routine that is doable for you regarding what you eat or quitting smoking or drinking. Make sure that, at stressful times of day, you have something in place to help you get through it: i.e. water, exercise, go for a walk, read, write, talk to someone.
4. Make sure you don't have to travel, or you don't have any social engagements for at least a month (but I would suggest three months) so that you can put your routine "in play."
5. Turn your routine into a habit. This takes longer and is perhaps the toughest part of making a health change. I'm sure you've

heard the general consensus that it takes about 21 days to form a habit. That might be the case for some people, but for those of us who have tried and failed so many times in the past, I would suggest that a habit might take about three months to become embedded. Stick to your routine for 90 days.

6. Keep things the same when it comes to what you eat, even if it means eating the same thing every single day. Same breakfast, same lunch, and same dinner (or with no more than two or three options for lunch or dinner). The reason for this is to eliminate or minimize the stress of figuring out what to prep. Of course, what you choose to eat has to be balanced and nutritious. I'm not a nutritionist or a personal trainer so I can't tell you what you should eat. But stick to the tried and true. Lean protein, lots of veggies, and small amounts of complex carbs.

7. Plan ahead. Make sure you reserve your Saturday or Sunday for grocery shopping and meal prep for the week ahead. When it comes to smoking and drinking, avoid potentially stressful situations or make sure you know what to say when your "smoking" buddy taps on your office door or your "drinking" buddy texts you about grabbing a few beers after work.

8. If you can afford to work with a personal trainer or a therapist or a health coach, get one—it can help you stay on track. But the internet is full of free info and videos that you can access that will help you. There are 12-

step groups or free groups and programs in your in your community that you can attend for support.

9. Whether you are trying to lose weight or stop smoking or drinking, I recommend exercise as a key addition to your "toolbox." Replace a bad habit with a good one. If age or a medical issue is a problem, start with something simple. The best exercise you can do is to walk. Your day is divided into 24 hours or 1,440 minutes. Out of those 24 hours, two-thirds or 16 hours are generally taken up by work and sleep. That leaves you with approximately eight hours or 480 minutes to play with (give or take). I suggest that out of those 480 minutes, you take 60 minutes and split them up into three 20-minute increments a day. Go for three 20-minute walks. Start with that and see where you end up after three months.

10. Finally, I recommend caution when beginning any new exercise routine or change in diet or eating plan, or if you are quitting smoking or drinking. Be sure to talk to your family doctor about what you intend to do, especially if you have high blood pressure, diabetes, or any other medical condition.

When I worked as a financial planner, my goal was to help families determine *their* goals. I helped them figure out how they could engage in life's big and exciting moments like buying a home or going on that big around-the-world adventure, while still being prepared for life changes that require a financial safety net: i.e. children's education, unemployment, health issues, etc. Many people don't want to think about those negative possibilities, but these are factors that we need to discuss in the financial wealth management arena. We work with families to provide them with the best possible advice and guidance to help them make the best decisions for their financial health. In order for us to do that, the families we work with have to do some interior reflection as they arrive at an exterior solution. Think about that.

Interior reflection leads to an exterior solution.
A similar approach can be used to help you with your eating issues. With that in mind, I have a simple writing exercise for you to do. I want you to describe three to five situations where you had an eating binge, or you overate, or you ate something unhealthy. Write down *the time, the place, and what you ate*. In the second column I want you to describe what happened before that unhealthy eating event.

What led up to it.
What were you feeling?
What were your emotions?
What were you doing?
What were you thinking about?

The purpose of this simple exercise is to get you thinking about what triggers your unhealthy habits. When you figure out the WHY, then you figure out WHAT you're going to do about it. The WHY is more important than the WHAT because it helps you come to terms with the stuff you've been hanging onto—all the baggage that affects you. Bad emotions lead to bad habits. Now, that's not to say that you can't ever feel negative emotions. You'll always have stress and stressful situations to deal with in your life. When I began Owning My Shit, it didn't mean I never felt shitty anymore. But even though you are experiencing a negative emotion, it doesn't mean you have to eat your way out of it.

Even though you experience a negative emotion, you don't have to eat, smoke, or drink your way out of it.

Once you've worked on pinpointing your triggers, write them down on a card, keep a note in your phone, write them in your journal or a notebook, or keep them posted on your fridge. By writing down what triggers you, you keep those triggers active in your conscious rather than buried deep in your subconscious. You stay mindful. And that's the key.

Good health is not only about motivation and commitment, it's also about education. One thing that made a big difference for me was learning about health and nutrition. When I began to learn, I began to lose my fear. There are a lot of great books, websites, and apps out there. Information is at our fingertips. There are plenty of online groups that are easily accessible. Read and learn, and you will figure out what works for you.

And of course, the other thing to keep in mind when you Own Your Shit where food, smoking, and alcohol are concerned is daily commitment. Whatever method of weight loss you choose—or "fat release" or diet or whatever you want to call it—is up to you. What I'm asking you to do is to own it.

Owning Your Shit is about making a commitment. That means making an *actual* commitment and sticking to it every single day. Otherwise, you will never reach your goal. It's as simple as that. As long as the outcome of your goal is in the future, you can always move that outcome down the line. *Oh, I'll just change my goal date to next month. That will give me more time to get my act together.* How many times have you told yourself that one?

As a wise person once said, "If you're tired of starting over, stop giving up."

Be brutally honest with yourself.

When I Owned My Shit, I admitted to myself I'd screwed up. I ate too much—too much sugar, fat, and bread—not just once or twice but consistently over many years. I drank too much, and I drank alcohol in situations that put others and myself in danger. I smoked too much, and I ignored the potential impact of smoking on my health. Remember the list of carcinogens I learned about when I was a kid in school? I shared that information with my parents all those years ago so that they would stop smoking. But I failed when it came to myself. I forgot about that little kid. I needed to remember him. His truth. When I say *be honest,* I'm not talking about beating yourself up. I'm talking about admitting that you are unhappy inside. That something is off, and you need to figure out what that is. Then you need to Own Your Shit. You are the key.

Recently I had a big argument with my older brother Greg. I couldn't help but notice that every time we had a family gathering and I arrived, a look would pass between my siblings. To say there was tension was an understatement. I realized that something was up, and I needed to address it. So, the week after one such family gathering, I called him up and asked him outright.

"What's going on? How come you all clam up when I walk into a room?" I asked.

"Well, to be honest, we always feel like you're judging us," Greg replied.

"What do you mean by judging you?"

"Because you're so regimented. Like you can't eat this, and you can't drink that, and you need to work out every day. It's like you don't know how to have fun anymore."

"Are you kidding me? I was obese and an alcoholic and a chain smoker. I was miserable."

"Well, you act like you're better than us now."

I couldn't believe what he was saying to me. He was 61 years old. Ten years older than me. Greg was the guy who took me in when I first moved out west. He bought me my first new pair of skates. He signed me up for junior hockey. He saved my butt on more than one occasion. He got me my first real job at Wasea Metal. He was my big brother, and he was telling me this.

"I don't think I'm better than you. I don't think I'm better than anyone," I said. "What I do think is that I am better today than I was five years ago. I'm better today because I'm fit and healthy and I care about everyone in my life and everything I put out into the world."

"Oh, here we go again," he muttered. "You know what? I feel sorry for you. It must be hard for Annie and Cole and Sidnee to live up to your lofty expectations. You want everyone to be perfect. That's not how life is, man. People should be able to live however they want. If they're happy, they're happy. Who cares if you're a few pounds overweight?"

"Let me ask you something," I went on. "If I had a heroin addiction would you help me?"

"Of course I would," he answered swiftly. "I would do whatever it took to help you."

"Then why didn't you reach out and help me when I was boozing and seventy pounds overweight?"

"That's not the same, Tim," Greg said. "What's wrong with having a beer or a burger every now and then?"

"Now and then is one thing," I counter. "But what I was doing to myself was self-destructive. Hell, don't you remember me telling you about the time when I was in Vegas with Annie and the kids, and I got so drunk I had to ask the driver to stop the car so I could puke my guts out on the street? How is that normal or fun? I was miserable, and I was well on my way to a heart attack."

Greg was silent on the other end.

"I'm not talking about being perfect. I'm talking about being healthy. I'm not talking about being some kind of male model. You think I fucking love doing two-hour workouts every day?" I shook my head. "I do it because I'm responsible for my life. I'm talking about being able to climb a flight of stairs without your heart racing. If you drive your car into the ground every single day and never change your oil, what are you going to end up doing to your car?"

"People aren't cars," Greg snapped back.

"You're right, people are more precious than cars." I countered. "I don't have expectations for my kids. I don't expect them to be perfect in life. I want them to be happy and healthy. I have expectations for myself. I take responsibility for my life and my mistakes, and I live my life every day Owning My Shit. I do it not only because I want to live a happy and healthy life, but because I want my kids to be proud of me. I want my kids to know that I care enough about myself and my life to live each day to best of my ability. That's what I care about."

I don't know if I got through, but I hope so. My brothers and sisters mean the world to me, and we've been through a lot together. I remain ever hopeful.

Not everyone is going to understand what you're doing when you decide to make that change, when you begin to Own Your Shit. Some of your friends and family and coworkers will cheer you on, while others might shut you out. But that is their reaction. You are only in charge of you and how you act. The only thing you can do is show by example. Owning Your Shit means living by example. It doesn't mean talking a good game. It doesn't mean being perfect. It doesn't mean judging others.

The pastor and author John Maxwell said, "Most people don't lead their life, they accept their life."

Think about that for a moment. Leading your life means taking responsibility and control. Not allowing others to dictate to you how to feel or think. You are responsible for that. And the great big secret is, you have a choice in this. You can choose to lead your life instead of sitting on the couch and letting your life lead you.

I think Grampy would have approved of Owning Your Shit. I think he understood the general premise and lived his life that way. Grampy was a heavy drinker for many years, but he quit. When I was growing up, I never saw him touch a drop of anything, not even beer. Grampy Owned His Shit. I wish I could have kept that in my heart and mind, when I'd begun spiraling out of control. I wish I'd had the wherewithal to stop myself before falling into such dark despair that I needed booze and beer to fill what was empty inside of me. I hope that one day, Greg and the rest of my family can understand that too.

Chapter 16

Negative or Positive? It's About Perspective.

*"The moment you change your perception, is the
moment you rewrite the chemistry of your body."*
—Dr. Bruce H. Lipton

"Mom, Dad! My life is falling apart!"

"What's wrong?" Annie asked.

Our daughter Sidnee looked devastated. Her eyes
were red and swollen, her normally rosy cheeks were
streaked with tears, and her lips trembled as though it
was all she could do to keep from breaking down.
Sidnee was on FaceTime with Annie and me. Annie
and I looked at each other with concern. What was
wrong with our usually happy daughter?

"They made all these changes to the team. And I
won't get enough playing time. And I won't be able
to get to the net to score as much. What am I going to
do?"

Annie and I exchanged a glance. We knew what
the answer was, we had to help Sidnee figure it out.
Sidnee was a great player. She played for the
Women's Soccer Team at Ryerson University. Her
first year there, she tied as lead scorer. She was elated

as were we. She'd worked very hard and had been playing since she was a kid.

We were proud of Sidnee's dedication to the sport. She even played in the winter months. Soccer in winter time is called Futsal. It generally follows the same rules but with a few differences: the game is played indoors, in a gymnasium, and there are five players on each side on the floor as opposed to 11 players on the grass in regular play. The ball is also smaller and heavier. Before Sidnee was accepted into Ryerson, she played for her high school team. One particular game stands out in my heart.

It was a snowy, cold day in January, but that didn't stop us from piling in the car and heading to the game. We had to get there early so Sidnee could warm up. We packed snacks for everyone—sandwiches, carrot sticks, cucumber slices, water, and homemade chicken broth to keep us warm. Cole came along too. Even though it was hockey season for Cole, he didn't have a practice or a game that day.

The gym was packed. Both teams had their family and friends there to cheer them on. The chants from both sides flowed back and forth in good natured rivalry. But when it came time to play, the athletes were all business.

Sidnee was on fire. Her foot work was a thing of beauty as she propelled herself down the court, shifting the ball from foot to foot. She was fast and nimble, weaving around the other team's defense and sliding in not one, not two, but six goals in the game. I was so proud of her. I couldn't help but remember my own childhood and my love of hockey, and how alive I felt when I stepped onto the ice and glided along, shifting the puck back and forth. Both Cole and Sidnee had inherited my love of sports, and I was happy they did.

Sidnee's team won the game, to great cheers. Cole high-fived Sidnee as they chatted excitedly about her performance. Annie and I beamed with pride.

Later, on the way home, as we continued to chat about the game, I asked Sidnee a question.

"You were on fire tonight, Smeag, more so than usual. What was going on in your head?" Smeagol, the alternate name for the character Gollum from *Lord of the Rings*, has been my nickname for Sidnee since she was a kid. Smeagol or "Smeag."

"I'm really starting to understand the value I bring to the team," Sidnee replied, a thoughtful smile on her face. "I'm starting to understand the difference I make when I perform at my best—the importance of taking those extra fifteen minutes every day to juggle the ball."

Annie and I exchanged a warm look.

Those lessons are priceless, and they would have never been taught had I not changed. Had I not begun to Own My Shit. Fortunately for both children, I did change. I was a lousy dad when I drank. Even though I changed and began to Own My Shit, I knew my kids had already been impacted by my drinking and bad behaviour. Life is all about learning, and Annie and I weren't done yet. There was more to learn. Sidnee and Cole learn from their mistakes and from the issues they encounter. In her FaceTime call to us now, Sidnee was experiencing one of those issues.

She was terribly upset by the changes on her soccer team at Ryerson. She had worked so hard to get that scholarship, and now it seemed like she was about to throw in the towel.

Annie and I listened closely to Sidnee's story, and to how stressed she was about the changes to her role on the team. She was now required to play numerous positions, but she wouldn't have as much time on the field, which meant fewer chances to score goals. It was time to help Sidnee reframe her point of view.

"What if an organization invites you to Toronto and pays you to be part of a team?" I asked.

"And when you get to Toronto, you meet twenty-three great young women, just like you, and have an instant community of friends in a city where you've never been before," Annie added.

Sidnee's expression began to change. She tilted her head, and her eyes looked thoughtful as she listened quietly.

"And you get paid to exercise and play a sport you love, while you study interior design." Annie said.

"And when you graduate," I continued, "you interview for a job at an interior design firm, and they look down at your resume and see all the wonderful things you accomplished and that you had a full scholarship and played soccer on the women's team for four years. Do you think the firm that interviews you is going to ask you how much playing time you had on the pitch?"

Sidnee's tears had dried up and she was chuckling now. "I get it."

"You get it?" Annie smiled. "What do you get, honey? Tell us."

"I was so stressed out about not having as much playing time to score that I forgot the big picture. I forgot all the good stuff of being on the team. And in the end, it won't really matter because I'm studying interior design."

"And the fact that you're learning so much by being a team player. Because that's how the world works—you have to be a team player," I said.

We spent the rest of the call talking about her term papers and upcoming exams. The storm had blown over, and Sidnee had a fresh new perspective on her experience.

Being a great parent is all about listening and helping your children formulate a healthy way of thinking about things. Sidnee's ego and pride were getting in the way of happiness. So, we gave her a nudge, a different way to process the information. She still had her scholarship and her friends, and less playing wouldn't affect her future career as an interior designer. Her playing time wasn't as important as she thought it was. Not when she realized the big picture.

If I hadn't begun to Own My Shit, those conversations with my children would never have happened.

Annie and Sidnee have an amazing bond, one of the finest and strongest relationships I have ever seen. What I have realized is that parenting isn't to procreate and put a person on this earth, the real purpose is to make a great community of citizens who engage with their families and their communities in a positive and nurturing way.

I went from eating junk food, binge drinking, smoking, and generally being "checked out" of my own family, blind to the fact that my children were watching and absorbing everything I did and said, to Owning My Shit.

I began to eat healthy, exercise, read every night, and truly engage with my children, and I saw the difference my changed actions made in them. When you show your children your commitment to a healthy and positive life, you are teaching them to look up to what you truly stand for, your value system. You are giving them the emotional nourishment they need to forge their own lives.

Chapter 17

My Hero.

"A mentor enables a person to achieve.
A hero shows what achievement looks like."
— John C. Mather

"If this kid steps out on the ice one more time, he could end up in a wheel chair."
The team doctor's words echoed in my head on our way home. I glanced at Annie beside me in the passenger seat. The anguish in her gaze mirrored my own. I swallowed the lump in my throat and glanced in the rear-view mirror at Cole in the back seat. He was texting someone on his iPhone. "Son," I began. "We're going to get through this."

Cole raised his head and smiled. "It's okay, Dad and Mom," he said. "It's going to be okay."

That's Cole in a nutshell. He reassures us. He smiles through adversity. Even when he's just gotten a punch to the gut.

Athletes live with the knowledge that they might be an injury away from the end of their careers. Some athletes sustain an injury and bounce back, while others never recover and are forced into early retirement. Cole was only at the beginning of his hockey career. He'd played two years of Junior B in British Columbia and one year of Junior A in Texas.

Cole had been offered a scholarship to attend SUNY Cortland in New York State while he was playing Junior A in El Paso. But as the playoffs approached, he'd begun to feel severe pain in his lower back. He experienced it on and off, but shrugged it off, as many people do when it comes to aches and pains. After all, Cole was in prime physical condition. He trained hard almost every day, ate healthy, and kept up his grades. If there is one word to describe my son's size, it's "strapping." He's six foot three and all muscle. A big guy. Much bigger than I am. Even though I still think of him as that towheaded kid shrugging his little shoulders when I asked him why he stole the pack of gum.

He was also the epitome of a team player. Any time one of his teammates was on the receiving end of an illegal check or a hit on the ice, Cole would throw down his gloves and go into protection mode. While he's a tough player on the ice, off the ice he's the easiest going fella around. His nickname is "Doc" because of his love of medicine, and because he's always ready to take care of his friends. One time, he called me after he and his teammates had gone out to tell me, "Dad, I have to drive the guys home, I'm the only one who wasn't drinking."

Cole knew all too well the dangers of drinking and driving. When I began to Own My Shit, I was able to be there for my kids. I was able to be present in their lives. To share my own successes and stumbles with them, and to show them you can change for the better. Luckily, my kids were young enough to learn that you can find light even in the darkest moments. They saw me at my worst, of course, and they were old enough to remember, so I know their scars run deep. But I also know that scars can heal.

They know that, to be a great leader, you must lead by example. They know that bringing your A-Game to everything you do—whether it's cooking a family dinner, running a marathon, or studying for final exams—is truly about taking responsibility. Giving your best effort. Owning Your Shit.

"Son, I'm proud of you," I said now, as I looked at him in the rear-view mirror.

"Thanks, Dad," he said. "I guess I'm going to have to figure out what to do next."

"Give it some time, honey," Annie said over her shoulder. "We only just found out and there are still more tests to do."

The team doctor referred us to a specialist who explained that Cole will need major surgery on his back to repair his ruptured disks. He faces a four-hour operation, followed by up to six months in recovery.

The bone doctor told us Cole will never be able to play hockey again. Annie and I are devasted for our son and the loss of his goals and dreams. Cole has played hockey from the age of five. You can imagine what hockey means to him. He lived and breathed it. Hockey wasn't just a sport, it was a way of life for Cole. He had his sights set on playing in Europe and having a solid career there. He's a great player, but he knows he's not NHL material. He has a few friends who were recruited into the NHL. Still, he was looking forward to moving to Europe, playing pro there, and travelling the world on the off season.

"Your son has the back of a seventy-year-old," the specialist bluntly told us. "He'll need titanium disks. He can't play hockey ever again."

The doctor also advised Cole to freeze a sperm sample because the surgery is so risky it could render him paralyzed and incapable of fathering children.

Cole is only 22 years old. But my son is already made of titanium. He recently enrolled in the sciences stream at Mount Royal University in Calgary. He's facing the unknown in the only way he knows how— with strength, fortitude, and a great sense of humour.

For that and for many other reasons—from having the courage to admit he stole a pack of gum when he was five years old, to texting his mom to pick him up after I got drunk at a hockey game, to being the guy who protects everyone else around him—my son is my hero.

Sometimes you don't need to look very far to find your heroes. Sometimes you can even look into your own heart.

Who do you admire and respect in your life? Why?

When you make a change, when you Own Your Shit as I have done, and as Annie, Sidnee, and Cole do every day, this is being heroic. You have an impact on other people. Everything you do. Everything you say. Everything you are.

You can be the hero in your life when you Own Your Shit every day.

Chapter 18

Take an Inventory.

Don't kid yourself. Be honest with yourself.
Take your own inventory.
— Jack Canfield

Every week when it's time to go grocery shopping, you take a quick inventory of the fridge, freezer, and pantry to see what you're running low on and what you have enough of. The same should be true when we think about making a significant change in our lives. When we take inventory of ourselves and our lives—whether it's about eating healthier, becoming more active, or trying to eliminate debt—it's important to take stock and figure out where you are now and where you want to be in a year, or two years, or five years down the road.

But how do you take stock? How do you take an inventory of YOUR life? As I said previously, when I hit my lowest point, driving my son home from a hockey game when I had been drinking, I did a lot of soul searching. I made the decision to change. I made the decision to Own My Shit. But I had to figure out how to get there, how to do that. I mentioned heading to the bookstore and perusing the self-help book shelves. It was the start that I needed. Reading about the experiences of others and how other people have changed can inspire you to do the same.

I read the book *Feel the Fear and Do It Anyway* by Susan Jeffers. Originally published in 1987, *Feel the Fear and Do It Anyway* is considered one of the seminal books in the area of self-growth and personal understanding. Susan Jeffers was an American psychologist who passed away in 2012, but in her lifetime, she became known as the Queen of Self-Help. She published 18 books in the self-help field and always drew from her own life experiences as well as her knowledge as an educator and psychologist in her writing.

The year I hit rock bottom was 2012, the same year that Susan Jeffers passed away. I took that as another sign that the universe was telling me to get my act together. I read that book from cover-to-cover and have since read it again and again. I continue to read books about self-understanding as I continue to reflect and re-evaluate my life. And yes, I continue to take inventory of my life. I want to help you do the same.

Remember the **Four Foundations of Owning Your Shit.**
1. **Health/Wellness**
2. **Relationships**
3. **Money/Career**
4. **Spirituality**

As you take an inventory of your life, take these four areas into consideration. How do you feel physically? Do you hop out of bed every morning ready to take on the day, or are do you trudge through the day armed with a double-double in one hand and a chocolate bar in the other? Do you enjoy a positive and nurturing relationship with your spouse, significant other, children, parents, friends, and coworkers? Or do you nurse grudges, resentments, and anger towards the important people in your life? Are you satisfied with your financial status? Do you feel comfortable because you've planned ahead and prepared for life's unexpected curveballs while still leaving some wiggle room for that big trip to Australia and New Zealand you've always wanted to take? Do you feel in balance in your spiritual life? Do you feel connected to the world around you and your place in it? Are you inspired to have a positive impact on others?

Here's an exercise for you: using the Four Foundations of Owning Your Shit as a guide — Health/Wellness; Relationships; Money/Career; Spirituality—make two columns on a sheet of paper or on your electronic device. In one column, write down the current state of your life, and in the other, write down where you want to be a year from now.

Based on the above exercise, make two more columns and focus on a list of specific things in your life that you want to improve. In one column, jot down what you want to improve, and in the other column, why you want to change those things.

The purpose of this exercise is to get you thinking about the "what" and the "why." The what, according to the Four Foundations of Owning Your Shit. How do you perceive your life in these four key areas? And where do you want your life to be a year from now in those four key areas? Then, using your answers as a guide, narrow it down a list of specific goals that you want to undertake.

You may also consider talking to a life coach, someone who can offer guidance, support, and honesty as you work on your "personal inventory" and what you want to change in your life—as well as helping you with all the practical stuff you'll need to figure out as you commit to the Owning Your Shit. There are many personal and life coaches out there. You may find that the only area of your life that needs work is financial/career, so consider a coach who specializes in finances. Or you might want to work on your health, in which case a personal trainer might be a good idea. When looking for a life coach or another kind of coach, remember to do your research. Read testimonials and reviews. Word of mouth is also important. Reach out to the people you know online and ask if they have ever engaged the services of a life coach.

You don't have to do everything all at once, like I did. You can pick one thing that you need to work on, and then move onto the next item on your list. At the end of the day, it's about awareness, responsibility, and positivity. It's about Owning Your Shit.

Chapter 19

Personal Goals and Career Goals
Instead of Number Goals.

*"If you want to be happy, set a goal that
commands your thoughts, liberates
your energy and inspires your hopes."*
—Andrew Carnegie

Every December 31, I write out my goals for the
upcoming year, print them out on a card, and
laminate it. On one side are my personal goals, and
on the other side, my business goals. I carry the card
with me in my wallet.

They aren't "goals" in the usual sense—i.e. "Lose
15 pounds by Summer," or "Run a 10k." They're
more like affirmations. But I like to use the word
goals because to me, they are what I aspire to and
what I strive for every day. They represent what I
want my highest self to achieve every day. And
they're also a reminder to Own My Shit.

I've been doing this since 2013.

Sometimes the goals make a second or third
appearance on my cards, because it feels right. The
laminated cards are a tool to keep me on track. But

the words are what's in my heart and what I am working to achieve.

I give myself a broad amount of time—one year—because I want the goal to become part of my daily routine. I don't give myself a year because I'm putting off getting these things done, but because I want to work on my goals every single day and beyond.

When it comes to work, if anyone reads this book from a professional standpoint, know that positional or title leadership is the weakest form of leadership. Servant leadership, in a full professional environment, where the client always comes first in everything we do, is the lesson I want everyone in the workplace to get.

Here is a list of the personal and career goals I have incorporated into my life since I began to Own My Shit. As you read down the list, you'll see that the goals are more like declarations, mantras, inspiring quotes, intentions. They are not quantifiable goals. Notice that my career goals do not reflect increasing my sales numbers or making more money. They are, in truth, a portable vision board with my philosophical outlook. They are a reminder to myself to Own My Shit every day.

2013
Personal Goals:
I am the best dad, husband, and professional I can be.
I will be true to myself and to others.
Career Goals:
I will say *yes* to the world.
I will make a positive impact on everyone.

2014
Personal Goals:
I will improve my self-conversations.
I will live in the moment.
Career Goal:
I will bring my A-game every day.

2015
Personal Goals:
A person who stands for nothing will fall for anything.
I will act with courage every day.
Career Goals:
Make a decision to make a decision.
Never negotiate with myself.

2016
Personal Goal:
A man who believes in nothing will fall for anything.
Career Goal:
Three great essentials to achieve anything—hard work, stick-to-it-ness and common sense.

2017
Personal Goals:
Never lie to myself.
I know what's right.
Career Goals:
90 per cent of the population will eventually work for the three per cent that never give up. (That's a

quote, but I can't remember who said it).
Make a decision to make a decision.

2018
Personal Goals:
Do what is right not what is easy.
A person who stands for nothing will fall for anything.
Career Goal:
Own Your Shit.

I want you to create a list of your personal and career or business goals. They don't have to be quantifiable. They can reflect your desire to change how you see the world. They can be an inspirational quote or just a common sense saying you remember from your childhood. These goals are philosophical in nature. They are meant to inspire and remind you every day to Own Your Shit.

Pick at least one of each and write them on a card or a sticky note or laminate them, but keep them with you. And every morning before your day gets busy, or as you are doing your 15-minute check-in, read them out loud.

Chapter 20

15 Rules for Owning Your Shit

"Success isn't just about what you accomplish in your life; it's about what you inspire others to do."
— *Unknown*

It's been about eight years since I started Owning My Shit. In that time, I've developed a set of 15 rules that I follow (some of them make an appearance on my laminated cards.) These rules help keep me grounded, they help keep me on track, and they help me stay focused on what is important. In other words, they help me Own My Shit. I believe they will help you too. By following these rules every day, you'll stay on track, stay focused, and stay mindful. These rules will help you achieve that all-important balance in life in those four foundations—your relationships, health, career, and spiritually.

As I ponder coming to the end of this incredible journey, I want to make sure that you understand the purpose of Own Your Shit.

I want you to know that being grateful and having humility in everything we do is the right attitude to have. We are in a constant state of learning in the four foundations of Own Your Shit—relationships, spiritual, health/wellbeing and career/financial. There is no order to the foundations—they are all equally important and if you practice Owning Your Shit every day, you'll see that keeping all four areas in balance is key.

Even for all coaching meetings in the workplace, helping each individual be the very best they can be (through proper rest, proper nutrition and proper exercise) should be the focus. Leaders in the workplace must know what is most important to every person they work with, from their spouse/partner, to their kids and/or parents, to their hopes and goals.

A true leader believes that everyone on their team would take a bullet for each other. Just as I would take a bullet for any member of my team. There is no one role more important than the other, they just pay differently. Each role comes with full respect. Make sure every voice has a voice, no matter what position they have.

When you achieve your team goals—when you reach each mountain peak—reinforce those beliefs with your team. The most important part is the getting there—the process—because that is what Owning Your Shit is all about. The WHY is far more important that the WHAT or the HOW. Share the why, develop the what, and make sure your team works diligently at the how.

In your personal life, remember your values, understand them, and practice them in your life. They will give you the energy to empower your life.

When it comes to your health, you must put on that proverbial oxygen mask first so that you can in turn help others. Redefine the meaning of selfish to mean focus on the self. Take care of yourself so that you can be of service to others.

When it comes to your family life, do everything it takes to make sure you never take your spouse or partner for granted. One night a week should be a date night, with phones away and no distractions present, so you can truly focus on each other. When it comes to parenting, you're never done teaching one lesson, because lessons are forever. Make sure you understand that your children can tell you anything. Do your very best to understand that, because if you close off that path, they will tell someone else, and you may not like the other person's answer. So make sure you are wide open and receptive to all conversations with respect, clarity and non-judgment.

Remember that the decisions you make today affect your spouse/partner, children, your grandchildren, your friends, and your workplace.

I began to share these 15 rules in my work presentations and public speaking at sales conferences, and I always get a positive reaction. I began to encourage my team members to try them. To incorporate them into their lives not just at work but at home.

Some of these rules might seem like common sense. But then again, the most obvious can be the hardest to stick to.

Tim Richardson's 15 Rules for Owning Your Shit.

1. Fuel your body.

Do you know anyone who owns a car that runs on bananas? Nope. A car runs on gasoline or a battery or both. So why would you put the wrong thing in your body? Why would you consume the kind of food that makes you feel sluggish and slow? Food is fuel. And we need to fuel our bodies in order to get shit done.

Owning Your Shit means respecting your body. It means understanding that you need good nutrition, good sleep, and exercise in order to embrace all the exciting new challenges on the road ahead. You need fuel for that. Make sure you get the right fuel.

2. Smile and say "hello", "please," and "thank you."

Seriously? That's a rule? You bet. Every day. Next time you're on an elevator, when everyone is facing forward, you turn around and say in a bright and cheery voice, "Good morning." I do that a lot. I get all kinds of reactions. Sometimes it's laughter, other times it's the wide eyes and the gaping mouths. But I don't mind. Sometimes it's a good way to break the ice. What if it's my last day on this earth? Am I going to spend it staring at the elevator panel or am I going to spend it interacting with people? If it's my last day in this wondrous thing we call "life," I'm going to say hi to everybody. I'm going to embrace being nice and yes, even silly.

3. *Dress for Success.*

As I mentioned earlier, I have some history with clothes. Heck, I admit it, I love tailored suits, pressed trousers, crisp shirts, and colourful ties. Hear me out. When I'm at the gym I wear shorts and a t-shirt, but when I'm at work, I dress in business attire. Many workplaces have casual Fridays or a more relaxed dress code, and that's fine. But when I began working as a financial advisor more than twenty years ago, I met with families to discuss how they would invest their life savings, so you can bet I did *not* show up wearing jeans and my faded Calgary Flames jersey. It just makes sense.

Owning Your Shit means being respectful of other people. And dressing like I'm going to a hockey game when I'm meeting with a couple to discuss everything from saving for their daughter's college education to planning their own funerals— well, that isn't Owning Your Shit, now, is it?

I remember a study where researchers asked a group of people which of the five senses they would least want to give up. The top answer: eyesight. There are plenty of psychological studies out there that determine how people perceive and process what they see. What does that tell you? It tells you people value what they can see. Which is why I think what you wear is important. It only takes seconds to register an impression about the kind of person you are interacting with. If you are in a profession like mine, be mindful of what you wear.

What does this have to do with Owning Your Shit? It has to do with respect for yourself and your coworkers and clients. Let's say you decided you weren't going to shower on the weekend. You just wanted to relax, watch movies on TV by yourself, and eat popcorn. Well, Monday morning rolls around and you decide not to shower. You haven't showered since Friday. You show up at work and people can literally smell you down the hall. Don't laugh. I've encountered this. Some people don't get the importance of personal hygiene. Now, you may have some kind of medical condition that contributes to excessive perspiration or bad breath, but there are things you can do to ameliorate those symptoms when you're in the public sphere.

What if you go out dancing with your friends on Saturday night and you get all dressed up? You wear a short, glittery dress, and sky-high heels. You get your hair done, big and fluffy like Farrah Fawcett, retro-style. You have a great time. But what if you decide to go to work dressed in your dancing outfit? Again, don't laugh. People do this.

Owning Your Shit means being respectful of others in the public sphere. What you wear and your personal hygiene are part of that.

4. Say "yes" to the universe (but know when to say "no" to the users and abusers).
Sometimes it's hard to say "no," so you end up saying "yes" to the coworker who asks you to help them with a presentation, and then you end up

doing the bulk of the work—and they don't acknowledge it. Or how about the neighbour who constantly borrows a tool from your house, and you say no problem, and then they never return it, and you have to go over there six months later and ask for it, and they can't seem to find where it is. Or there's that friend who never seems to have their credit card, debit card, or any cash when the restaurant bill arrives, so they ask you to cover them "just this once." You say no problem, and then every time you see them, there's a sudden case of amnesia about that 40 bucks.

Owning Your Shit doesn't mean allowing people to take advantage of you. It means taking responsibility for yourself and your actions. There are toxic people everywhere, but if we allow toxic people to control our lives and take advantage of us—then that's on us, not them. It's up to us to say *no*.

But what about your friend who's recently gone through a divorce and asks you to stay over because she doesn't want to be alone? Or what if your boss asks for a volunteer at the Monday morning meeting to go to Thunder Bay next month to give a presentation, and you hem and haw and hesitate, and someone beats you to it? Or what if your spouse asks you on the spur of the moment to go on a weekend getaway, and your reply is an automatic *no*, without even talking it over? Sometimes saying yes is the right thing to do.

Say *no* and be honest when someone is taking advantage of you. Say *yes* to the universe when someone you care about is hurting and needs emotional support. Say *yes* when it could mean an exciting new path in your career. Say *yes* to loved ones who want to spend time with you. Owning Your Shit means being honest with others and with yourself. If you consistently say *no* when it matters, then the universe will stop asking.

5. *Set goals that transform you from the inside out.*

I never talk number goals with my team. We never set sales goals or money goals. Instead I ask, "How are you more valuable today than you were 12 months ago?" Setting goals is about "growth mindset." You can shoot for those high sales and money goals, but if you're miserable, then what good is it? Remember, I was making plenty of money by 2012. I was golden. I'd grown up from a kid who grew up in Middle Sackville, New Brunswick in a broken-down house with no number and rats in mud cellars to being a financial planner who then became a Regional Director for a large corporation and was making six figures. I owned a big house and a nice car, and I went on fancy vacations. But there was something missing. I wasn't Owning My Shit.

Whatever career you are in—always be learning. Expand your world. Make a reading list of books you really want to dig into, join a book club, or take a few workshops—either career or hobby-related. Or maybe go to back to school; find a distance education program, or carve out some time for a night class. You can always add more tools to your toolbox, and that's what goals are all about. Adding value to your life.

Owning Your Shit means expanding your horizons and not just going through the motions of your career. If you're tired of your job, do something about it: visit human resources; talk to your boss about taking on a special project; pitch an idea to your team; look online for other positions; or take stock and think about something else that you might enjoy doing and maybe transform a hobby into a career. (But make sure you educate yourself about it and take the right steps to make the transition.)

6. *Always bring your A-Game.*

Your A-game has nothing to do with being the champ. It doesn't mean "pushing through" even when you're exhausted or have a cough that sounds like a dog barking. It means taking care of yourself, so you can put your best into your work, your home life, your family. It means getting proper rest, nutrition, and exercise daily. If you wake up in the morning and you know you're just not in the game—maybe you're feeling dizzy or you have a sore throat—then call your supervisor or boss and be honest. If you can't call in sick, then do your best and re-evaluate how you can make changes in your routine or your work schedule to improve your energy levels and/or get your health on track. If you constantly have a cold or indigestion or you're always feeling tired, even after getting eight hours—then there is something deeper that you need to look into.

7. *Be the eternal optimist.*

Have you ever met a "downer?" It takes just as much effort to be pissed off as it does to be happy. Probably more. You know those people on social media? The ones who are always griping and complaining about drivers, or that guy at the grocery store, or their professor, or politics. When you read those posts, how do you feel? Do you want to unfriend them because all they spout is negativity? Don't let that person be you. I'm not saying you have to fake it all the time. I'm saying that if you have a positive outlook on life, then it doesn't matter what the guy at the grocery store does or says. You are in charge of how you react to what you experience every day. You can either react negatively or you can have a more proactive approach.

8. *Live in the moment.*

Our smartphones have outsmarted us. We no longer interact with people anymore. We only interact with whatever technological gadget we have in our hands. We are literally going through life with our heads down, staring at our phone screens. If you're out for dinner with a friend or your spouse or your kids, don't look at your phone, look at the people sitting across from you. Look people in the eye and talk to them. Share your thoughts and feelings. Share your life. Your life is not in your phone, it's all around you. You need to live in the present moment and interact with living, breathing, beings around you, not with the various apps on your phone. Owning Your Shit is about making good use of technology, not allowing technology to use up all our time and energy.

9. Give empathy.

Every day I want to put my best out there. Some days people might need my experience, other days it's my expertise—and some days they need my empathy. My ability to put myself in their shoes and understand the world from their perspective. Those days are the most precious and help to define you as a person. Owning Your Shit means being able to put aside your shit for a while in order to offer comfort and support to those who are going through a rough patch.

10. Over-communicate.

Never underestimate communication. When we communicate with our egos, we tend to *mis*communicate or *mis*inform, and we "miss" the chance of saying what we truly mean and want. Owning Your Shit means being truthful, straightforward, honest. Being evasive or unclear is only going to cause trouble. This is what I refer to as "over-communicating." By that, I mean communicate over and above your ego. Own Your Shit when you communicate.

When your spouse asks you if something's bothering you and you say "nothing," but you're actually kind of angry that she changed her mind about going on the cruise for your vacation, you are not communicating with your mind and heart but with your ego. Communicate with your heart and you will get your point across. I'm not saying have a fit and yell and stomp your feet until you get your way. I'm saying let her know that you were looking forward to the cruise and ask if she would be open to discussing it or an alternative for your vacation.

One day my son comes up to me and asks, "Hey, Dad what are you doing tomorrow night?" Now, I know my son doesn't really care what plans I may or may not have on a Saturday night. I know he wants something—whether it's to borrow my car, or borrow some money, or ask me to take him somewhere. So, I say to him, "Hey, Cole, I thank you for asking, but why do you want to know?" Be clear. Be direct.

One of the problems we have in relationships with our loved ones and in the workplace is that we don't communicate clearly. We'll reply to a client's email instead of setting up a coffee or lunch meeting with them so that we can clearly explain the value we can offer them for the fee we are charging. Don't just shoot off an email listing your fees, because it can be *mis*interpreted or *mis*understood, and the person on the other end won't get the big picture.

11. Life is but one shot.

My dad passed away recently, and I miss him every day. He was a tough man. He had a harsh way of teaching you a lesson, but he was a good man and he worked hard. He was married to my mom for 30 years before they divorced, and in retrospect, I can honestly say that the divorce was a good thing for them. It was devastating for us kids, but that was also because Mom took us out west.

My dad ended up in a rebound relationship for a while, and then he married a friend of the family. Ironically, one of Mom's closest friends. They had a good life and he mellowed. I never saw him happier than he was in the last twenty years of his life. I'm happy that he found contentment and inner peace in his life before he passed on.

I hope Dad is enjoying a mug of cider with grandfather William (his dad) and Grampy Dos (Mum's dad), and I look forward to raising a glass with him when it's my turn to cross into the Great Unknown. I truly hope that we are all going somewhere wonderful after we die. But just in case, isn't it a good idea to make the most of the time we have here? I'm glad my dad realized that. I hope you do too.

12. *Unload preconceived notions.*

Never assume what someone's intentions are before you speak with them. You might think someone is angry at you or wants to take advantage of you, but maybe they just want to talk. Or maybe they want to tell you a funny story. Always be openminded. Then make your decisions based on someone's actions.

One day, I got a call from a friend whose husband had a brain tumor and was undergoing chemotherapy. I got the call while I was out of my office, and my assistant took the message. I asked my assistant how my friend sounded on the phone.

Did she sound upset or depressed? Was she crying? I assumed she was letting me know that her husband had passed away or was back in the hospital. I returned her call, preparing for the worst, and I found out that she was inquiring about a charity golf tournament that we were having. She wanted to buy tickets for her and her husband. Don't go through life assuming the worst about people or situations, or you will always carry a lump of anxiety in your gut. Owning Your Shit means not jumping to conclusions about your new manager or the new landlord of your apartment building or the couple who moved in next door with that Pitbull. Always keep your mind and heart open because you never know what's on the other end of a phone call.

13. Take that extra 15 minutes.

Before I begin my work day, I take 15 minutes to "check in" with myself. You might meditate, you might jot a few thoughts in a journal or a notebook. You might do some jumping jacks or just make yourself a cup of tea. You might just close your eyes and envision yourself having a good day. Whatever you choose to do, check in with yourself at the beginning of the day—it's called "being mindful" and it helps keep you grounded before you get pulled in all those different directions.

14. Important conversations with yourself.

Sometimes in life you need to have those "big" talks with yourself. You need to ask yourself if this is what you really want. If it's important to your life. And yes, you need to ask yourself, "Am I Owning My Shit?" Because you can get advice from many wise people—friends, family, partner, spouse, kids, parents, counselors, spiritual advisors etc.—but at the end of the day, the most important person you need to communicate with is yourself.

Ten years ago, I had the most important conversation of my life—with myself. I had to face some hard truths about my excesses—drinking, eating, not engaging with my family, overworking. I started to Own My Shit and I have never looked back. But I continue to have those important conversations every so often, because I need to understand where I'm at and how far I've come.

15. *Forgive yourself.*

Remember the purpose of Owning Your Shit is not about beating yourself up. It's about taking responsibility. It's not about turning yourself into a perfect human being or a martyr or a saint. It's about being true to what is important in your life. But it's also about forgiving yourself. You can't Own Your Shit if you hold onto that guilt and pain and anger at yourself. You have to forgive yourself. That's the only way to move forward.

Epilogue

A New Beginning.

"What you do makes a difference, and you have to decide what kind of difference you want to make."
—Jake Goodall

Before I began Owning My Shit, I was teetering on the edge of a cliff, looking down into a black chasm. I could have fallen off that cliff. I could have alienated and lost everyone and everything important to me.

I will never forget Annie's words to me back in 2011 on that trip to Vegas with the kids. "This is getting really old, Mr. Richardson."

Annie helped pull me back from the edge of that cliff. Annie is the strongest woman I know. She amazes me each and every day, and I love her with everything that I am.

Owning Your Shit is also about love—love of self, love of your family and friends, love of community, and love of spirit.

This book is not just about my life story and how I want to help you Own Your Shit. It's also about how I came to truly appreciate how wonderful it is to have a partner in life who stands with you in the bad times and celebrates the good times.

Annie is my partner.

This is our love story.

It's weekly date night. Annie and I are at Mercato's for dinner before heading out to see the Calgary Flames play at the Saddledome. Annie sighs with pleasure as she takes a sip of wine. It's her favourite, Chateau Neuf de Pape. I smile as I pick up the bottle of San Pellegrino and fill my glass with the sparkling water. We polished off our shared appetizer of prosciutto-wrapped asparagus. The waiter arrives with our entrée: Bistecca Fiorentina, a 26-oz steak seasoned with garlic, salt, and pepper and then grilled to a perfect medium rare and served with lemon juice and arugula along with grilled vegetables.

"This looks sooooo good!" Annie says with a grin. Her golden hair catches the candle's light. She looks beautiful in anything, but tonight she's dressed casually in a grey cashmere turtle neck tucked into fitted black jeans. I'm wearing a navy, V-neck sweater and a pair of khakis. If anyone happened to glance over at our table, they would see a relaxed, happy couple, fit and vibrant, enjoying each other's company. And that would be the truth. We are all of those things and more.

"You look soooo good," I tell her with a wink.

She waves a finger at me. "Oh, behave," she says in her best Austen Powers voice.

We tuck into our dinner, the conversation flowing between us. We talk about the latest book I'm reading and the latest movie she wants me to go see. We flirt. We joke. We have fun.

"Remember our first date?" I ask her with a grin.

"I remember." She laughs. "I remember it almost didn't happen…"

It was my last summer as apprenticing as a pro, teaching golf at club. I'd logged in three years, and I needed another two years to get my pro licence and be able to run my own golf course. But I was looking to get out. I was 21 years old, and my friend Murray, who was a member, gave me my first job in sales. He sold multicolored hangers to dry cleaning businesses so their customers would remember which cleaner they went to just by the hanger. It was a smart way to create a connection with the customer. Murray was another early mentor of mine. The first day on the job, he wrote me a cheque and handed me the keys to one of the company trucks. He told me to go buy a couple of couple of nice suits and then fill up the truck with hangers from the warehouse, drive to B.C. and not come back until I sold them all. I sure did.

"Kid, you're a natural," Murray said, slapping me on the back. "The way you talk to people—you'll clean up in the dry-cleaning biz. Get it?" He chuckled at his own joke.

While I was working at Douglasdale, I'd frequent Curley's Bar and Grill with a bunch of golf pro buddies of mine from the summer. Tuesday nights were Toonie Tuesdays, meaning drinks were on special for two dollars. Most of my friends were club members, and they were all about twenty years older than me and married, with a lot of money. They would tease me about being a young buck. I certainly was. I dated a lot and the gals liked me. I was cocky, I was tanned, I wore the golf pro "uniform"—a white

Douglasdale golf shirt with the company logo printed over the breast pocket and pressed beige slacks—as if it were made for me. And I was in good shape because I spent all day out on the course.

We were just sitting down at our table at Curley's on one of those Tuesday nights when I looked up and saw her. Blonde hair, brown eyes, and beautiful.

She was new at Curley's, and I'd seen her about. Every time I saw her, I felt compelled to talk to her, but for some reason I didn't approach her. I guess it was because she was always in work mode, moving around from table to table. Friendly but definitely not flirty. And she was the most efficient server I'd ever seen. But I wanted to ask her out, so I asked my friends to wish me luck.

"Good luck," they cackled from the table. I gave them the finger and strolled up to her.

"Hi there. I'm Tim. I work over at Douglasdale Estates Golf Club."

"Yeah, I know," she said, not sparing me so much as a glance as she began cleared the table of dirty plates and cutlery, stacking them into a dish bin.

"You're Anne Marie, right?"

She stopped clearing and looked at me. "Yes, but you already know that because I've served you a few times already. And it's on my name tag."

I chuckled, hoping I sounded cool. "It's a pretty name."

"It's a pretty *common* name," she said as she picked up a fork from the floor and tossed it into the bin.

"I don't think there's anything common about

you, Annie. Listen, how about we go out sometime?"
Please turn around and say yes. Please turn around and say yes.

She turned around.

Yes!

"Sorry, Tim, but I don't go out with womanizers."

Shit!

"What makes you think I'm a womanizer?"

She lifted a fine blonde eyebrow and placed her hand on her hip, leaning into the side of the table. "Um, I've seen you work the room."

"Oh, well, that means you noticed me then?"

She rolled her eyes and took out a clean, damp rag and began to wipe down the table. "Look, Tim, I'm here to make extra money while I work my way through school. I'm not interested in playing games. OK?"

Without giving me another look, she hefted the overloaded dish bin and hauled it through the swinging doors to the kitchen.

Damn!

I went back to my table and had to put up with some good-natured ribbing from my friends. I rarely ever got shut down, but Annie was one tough cookie.

Five years later, on a sunny Saturday afternoon, I was playing on the course where I was now a member. I was doing well in the dry-cleaning business and feeling pretty proud of myself. Then I see Anne Marie on the course with a group. It starts raining and everyone makes their way back to the club house. I'm just about to walk up to her and say hello when I see a guy from the group approach her and wrap his arm around her. They leave right away.

Damn!

Two weeks later I'm sitting in the stands at a Calgary Stampeder's football game and I see Anne Marie again, sitting just a couple of rows down from me.

This has got to be fate.

I get up and approach her to say hello. She's sitting beside another girl her age. A pair of big, dark sunglasses are perched on her nose, but I can tell she's surprised to see me. "Don't you think it's strange that we haven't seen each other for five years," I say, "and now here I cross paths with you in a packed stadium of thirty-five thousand people? "

She laughed at that.

Yes!

"I saw you the other day at the golf course, but I didn't get a chance to say hi. You left with some guy... boyfriend?"

"Oh, Rudy?" She smiled and waved her hand. "He's my cousin. He was visiting from out of town."

I smiled back. I couldn't help but notice she seemed way more relaxed than she'd been when she was a student waiting tables at Curley's. And beautiful, of course. Her blonde hair was all wavy and a bit longer, and she was tanned and wearing a sexy, lacy blue top with spaghetti straps and white shorts.

"So, if you're not seeing anyone, how about we go out sometime?"

She hesitated and her smile faded a bit. "Um, I'm actually sort of seeing someone." She gave a little nod and cleared her throat, throwing a quick glance at her friend.

I nodded back. Trying not to look completely dejected, I said a quick, "Okay, see ya in five years maybe." And waited for the awkward laughter.

Fuck!

A week later, I was back at Curley's with a few friends after playing a few rounds of golf and there was Anne Marie sitting at a booth with the same gal I'd seen her with at the football game.

Unfortunately, some dude with glasses and a buttoned-up shirt was sitting across from them. It looked like they were interviewing him for a job. He had a sheen of sweat across his brow and kept taking sips of his water. Whoever he was, he sure as hell wasn't her boyfriend.

"Okay, this it," I said under my breath. I strolled up to their booth and leaned in with a big smile on my face.

"Hey, Anne Marie. So, I haven't seen you in five years and then I see you three times in less than two weeks. Gotta be karma or something." I grinned. "Let's have dinner tomorrow."

She glanced at her wide-eyed friend and then at glasses guy, and then she cleared her throat and it looked like she was about to shoot me down again.

"I'll make you dinner," I offered quickly.

"What? Dinner? I'm not going to your place." She shook her head.

"Okay, whatever." I threw up my hands and walk back to my booth. My friends are shaking their heads at me. I chuckled good naturedly but inside, I couldn't figure it out. I couldn't figure *her* out. Why couldn't she go out with me just once?

A few minutes later, she shows up at our booth and asks to talk to me privately.

"I just wanted to apologize for the way I acted with you."

"Hey, it's okay." I nodded. "What happened to Mr. Glasses?" I asked.

"Oh ..." She blew out a breath. "He was a blind date that both Susan and I connected with through a dating service, and we decided to meet up to see which one he liked better, but neither of us was into him." Her cheeks pinkened at that.

"So, you came over to tell me that you were on a blind date?"

"Noooo, not exactly." She blushed and she looked so adorable, I had to slip my hands into my pockets to keep from hugging her.

"Do you still want to take me out?"

"I do," I said gazing into her eyes intently. She opened her purse, taking out a small notebook and a pen. She hesitated and then a smile curved her lips as she wrote something down, tore out the sheet and handed it to me.

I glanced at it and saw it was missing the last number. "You forgot the last number."

"Well, if you really want to go out with me, you can figure it out."

With that, she sauntered out of the pub with her friend.

Son of a gun if her number didn't end with a nine.

Our first date was at my apartment. My idea of making dinner back then was ordering from Dominos, so as we were lounging on the carpet, eating our pizza while she gazed around with that same gleam in her eye that she had at the restaurant.

My entire apartment was completely decorated in black and white. White walls. Black leather couch. White carpet. Black lacquer dining table and chairs. Black stereo. White stereo stand. My CDs were neatly stacked in a black CD tower in alphabetical order. There wasn't a dust bunny to be found. After growing up in a rundown house with no number and rats in the mud cellar, I vowed I would make enough money to live the way I wanted to live and have everything in the exact way I wanted.

"You sure like everything in a certain order, don't you?" Anne Marie said, a teasing note in her voice.

"Yeah, I do. I like having everything neat and tidy."

"I'll say." She pulled a CD out of its slot in the tower and set it on the carpet. "Hmm... what would happen if things got a little disordered?" She giggled as she pulled another CD out and set it down beside the first one.

"Hey, I just organized those the other day."

She giggled again, and she began to pull more CDs out and dropped them onto the carpet. She was having a grand old time, messing up my collection. There was only one thing I could do. I wrapped my arms around her and kissed her.

We've been together ever since.

"Aren't you glad I messed up your CD collection?" Annie giggled as she picked up her wine glass again.

"Yes." I chuckled. "I'm especially glad you finally said yes to going out with me after so many rejections."

"Well, you had to earn it," she laughed again.

"Are you glad you finally said yes, Mrs. Richardson?" I ask her softly.

She tilted her head to one side, and her warm brown eyes glowed in the candlelight. "Yes," she replied. "I'm very glad, Mr. Richardson."

After dinner, as we sipped our coffee, I reached out and took Annie's hand in mine.

I couldn't help but give thanks to the universe for giving me the privilege and honour of being Anne Marie's husband. My life would be very different now if I hadn't taken that first step—if I didn't start Owning My Shit.

Now, I live by it every day.

Make a decision to make a decision.

If you screw up, don't give up. Just start again.

Don't negotiate with yourself.

Hold yourself to a higher standard, because if you don't, no one else will, either.

I cherish every moment I have with Annie. She stuck by me and helped me through the toughest time in my life. I cherish Cole and Sidnee. I cherish my family and friends. I cherish my life, and I am thankful, so thankful for everything I have.

I'm here. I'm ready to embark on the next phase. I want to help you realize that you can do what I did and what I continue to do every single day.

Let's get started.

Author Bio:

Tim Richardson is a regional director in the financial services industry who loves to share his motivational wisdom on stages across North America. When he doesn't have his nose in a book, he enjoys spending time working on himself at the golf course or in the gym. Tim lives with his wife and two young adult children in Calgary, Alberta.

CPSIA information can be obtained
at www.ICGtesting.com
Printed in the USA
LVHW090217050719
623197LV00001B/8/P